Japan

Berlitz Publishing Company, Inc.
Princeton   Mexico City   Dublin   Eschborn   Singapore

Text:	revised text by Dennis Kessler; original text by Jack Altman
Editor:	Richard Wallis
Photography:	Dennis Kessler except for pages 4, 23, 27, 37, 88, 137, 143, 162, 167, 168, 172, 177, 197 (inset), 201
Cover Photo:	Dennis Kessler
Photo Editor:	Naomi Zinn
Layout:	Media Content Marketing, Inc.
Cartography:	Ortelius Design

The author wishes to thank Yoshimi Mizuno and Nozomi Oishi of
the Japan National Tourism Organization for their assistance and information in preparing this book. Generous support and assistance
was received from the excellent Japanese Inn Group, specifically
1999 president Mr. K. Tobita, and 1998 president Mr. I. Sawa. Finally, very special thanks to Allison Perry for invaluable support above
and beyond the call.

*Although the publisher tries to insure the accuracy of all the infor-
mation in this book, changes are inevitable and errors may result.
The publisher cannot be responsible for any resulting loss, incon-
venience, or injury. If you find an error in this guide, please let the
editors know by writing to Berlitz Publishing Company, 400
Alexander Park, Princeton, NJ 08540-6306.*

ISBN 2-8315-7219-3
Revised 1999 – Second Printing May 2000

Printed in Italy
020/005 RP

CONTENTS

Maps

Kyoto 92, Nara 115, Western Honshu & Shikoku 148,
Kyushu 159, Tohoku & Hokkaido 174

• A ☞ in the text denotes a highly recommended sight

Japan

JAPAN AND ITS PEOPLE

Its famous bullet trains zip through the country at up to 300 km (186 miles) per hour. Its factories feature the latest generation of industrial robots that don't eat, don't sleep, and never strike. Its high-tech consumer electronics companies have placed affordable—and notoriously reliable—electronic products in households around the world.

But peel back a layer and a different picture starts to emerge. In many ways, Japan is not yet a truly modern country. Its social roots still lie deeply in its past as a feudal society of countless closely knit agricultural communities dominated by a small political elite.

Japan is still trying to define its place in a world in which it is constantly accused of being an economic whale but a political minnow—just one of the pieces of the puzzle that is modern Japan. Truly, any examination of political, economic, and social issues invariably raises more questions that it answers. One pattern that quickly arises is an apparently never-ending series of contradictions.

> **The Japanese bow to each other when they meet. But they won't be at all dismayed if you offer to shake hands instead.**

Where lies the real Japan? Simply put, it is all around you. For Japan is truly a kaleidoscope of lifestyles and images, local cultures and beliefs: the rice farmers in rural heartlands and the subway millions of teeming Tokyo; the Zen Buddhist monks and the fad-obsessed teenaged fashion victims; the solemn temple ceremony or the hellish din of the pachinko parlor; exquisite temple architecture or all-pervasive soulless concrete apartment buildings. All represent different, often contradictory, facets of the greater whole that is Japan—one of the world's most intriguing countries.

The meticulous planning that helped the country to rise from the ashes of World War II to become the world's second largest economic power has in the 1990s created a prolonged slump. A people so justifiably famous for hospitality, politeness, and respect also produced an army whose brutality during its occupation of Southeast Asia during the war remains a stumbling block to "normal" international relations. A society whose indigenous religion centers on nature worship for decades has tolerated appalling environmental damage—commercially exploiting its own nature reserves for timber, lining river banks and beds with concrete, and filling its air, water, and land with dioxins and other pollutants.

These are just some of the issues facing anyone wishing to "understand" Japan—if such a thing is indeed possible. After all, the Japanese themselves are constantly analyzing their own nature. In fact, they have devised the subject of *Nihonjinron* (the "theory of Japaneseness"), books on which sell millions of copies each year and cover such bizarre topics as the unique chemistry of Japanese blood, the special configuration of the Japanese brain, and other examples of what supposedly sets them apart from the rest of humanity.

Unquestionably, few visitors will come to Japan truly free of preconceptions. There is no shortage of stereotypes: the beleaguered workaholic salaryman, the exotic geisha, the long-suffering Japanese housewife. Regardless of the degree of truth in these images, the secret of any successful and satisfying exploration of Japan is to cast aside preconceived notions and come with an open mind.

This is certainly a challenging task, but the rewards for doing so are the myriad windows and doors into this fascinating country that will open for you. For despite its reputation for homogeneity, Japan is in fact a country of astonishing contrasts.

Despite the concrete sprawl of Japan's postwar urban development, you can still find tranquillity in a brilliant-green, moss-covered temple garden or in the alcove of a traditional restaurant with its *tatami*-mat flooring, shielded from the other guests by *shoji* (paper screens)—remnants of a not-so-distant past.

The Japanese themselves have no trouble wandering easily from one such context to another. Home again after a hard day at the office, the director of a consumer electronics company who wears a business suit

Time-honored traditions: local devotees write wooden prayers at Nikko's famous Toshogu Shrine.

in downtown Tokyo sees nothing strange about buying cigarettes from a machine located inches from a sacred Shinto shrine. Once home, he might change into a garish velour leisure suit or an elegant *yukata* (light cotton kimono), the traditional informal attire for both men and women.

Even Japan's disaffected youth, normally sporting dyed hair, nose-rings, and torn T-shirts (and whatever else constitutes the latest street fashions to be slavishly copied), will attend an important festival in an expensive traditional costume, perhaps indicating that, despite their parents' concerns about their superficial appearance, some old values have not been entirely abandoned.

Everywhere you go, you're likely to find this constant contrast between old and young, traditional and modern, past and present. Oftentimes, these polar opposites come together: Ise-Shima, the most sacred of all sanctuaries of Shinto (Japan's ancient, nature-worshipping indigenous religion) reinforces Japan's profoundly intimate links with the Sun Goddess and her grandson, the God of the Earth. Although it was established some 1,700 years ago, the main shrine you'll see today was erected in 1993. Unlike Christianity's massive gothic cathedrals, designed to convey a strong sense of permanence, this austere wooden structure is dismantled every 20 years and replaced by a new one. Since Japan's Shinto deities are believed to permeate the natural surroundings—in this case, a beautiful cedar forest—the man-made shrine is just there for the fleeting present moment.

This strong sense of transience and impermanence has doubtless arisen as a natural response to Japan's devastating geography and seismology. The string of islands that make up Japan is in fact a highly volatile archipelago dotted with volcanoes and regularly subjected to earthquakes and typhoons. Over the ages, the Japanese built everything of wood—and then waited fatalistically for them to burn down, collapse, or be blown away in one catastrophe or another, after which they commenced another cycle of rebuilding.

Not until a 20th-century Western architect, Frank Lloyd Wright, arrived in Tokyo to build

You will find frequent opportunities to marvel over the skilled craftsmanship of Japan's artists.

the earthquake-resistant Imperial Hotel was it considered possible — let alone desirable — to attempt to defy the ravages of nature.

Today, office blocks and apartment buildings are of course constructed with modern materials. However, the failure of many to withstand the powerful 1995 Hanshin earthquake that struck the Kobe area exposed the inadequacy of many construction methods and standards. The postwar obsession with comfort, convenience, and the latest electronic gadgetry has led most Japanese to forsake the traditional, simple, and elegant house of wooden walls, heavy tiled roofs, tatami-mat floors, and sliding panels for a modern "Western-style" house designed to exchange the austerity of the past for the prosperity of the future.

Japan lies on the Pacific Rim at the edge of Asia. It comprises four main islands, dominated by Honshu, with Hokkaido to the north, Shikoku across the narrow Inland Sea, and Kyushu to the southwest. Together with more than 3,900 smaller islands from northeast to southwest, the archipelago would stretch from Montreal all the way down to Miami.

> **Communal baths are common at Japanese inns and resorts. Soap up, scrub down, and shower off completely before you get in the tub.**

The climate correspondingly varies from the snowy northern tip of Hokkaido, which offers excellent skiing, to the subtropical region of southern Kyushu and Okinawa, with its popular coral reefs. Honshu, the main island and home to Tokyo, Kyoto, and Osaka, enjoys a temperate climate of unusually distinct seasons: bitter winters and hot, humid summers. Winters are milder and sunnier on the Pacific coast, permitting a welcome double crop of the all-important staple — rice.

One advantage of living on what amounts to a long string of volcanoes is the proliferation of *onsen,* or hot springs. The profusion of these natural phenomena has long made "taking the waters" an integral aspect of Japanese culture and lifestyle. Onsen range from naturally occurring outdoor rockpools to large hotel-style resorts designed for guests to cast aside the stresses of the outside world as they soak for hours in communal hot tubs. Spending at least one night in a traditional Japanese inn-style onsen is an experience every visitor should enjoy.

The jagged mountain ranges and dense forests leave less than two-fifths of the country suitable for habitation and farming. Japan's 120 million inhabitants have to crowd the coastal plains and the narrow river valleys despite a total land area greater than Germany's. In terms of the ratio of population to usable land, Japan is the most densely populated country in the world.

Does such crowding account for Japan's legendary tradition of politeness, self-discipline, and resigned acceptance? In some ways, this is the only way to make an intolerable situation somehow manageable. Visitors are amazed at the apparent harmony that reigns amid the bustle of city life, especially the absence of the levels of violent crime that seems endemic in much of the rest of the developed world.

But as with many theories, the reality is less straightforward. Crime rates are rising, especially violent crimes involving the young. Even sexual assaults are increasing—although this might reflect a reduction of social stigma in what remains a deeply conservative society, where previously the number of reported incidents was severely constrained.

Still, Japan remains one of the safest countries in the world to live or visit. Historians and sociologists like to explain it all as a continuation of the feudal spirit of rigidly reinforced social hierarchies, with company presidents as latter-day shoguns and middle management as reincarnated *samurai* warriors. Whatever the validity of such parallels, the prevailing social harmony clearly owes much to the homogeneity of the Japanese population. From a stock of Mongolian, Chinese, Korean, and perhaps also Malay settlers, the country has had several thousand years to develop a solidly unified ethnicity. Japan has never experienced the kind of large-scale immigration or even—until the postwar US occupation from 1945 to 1952—foreign invasion that has made for social conflict in other countries.

But this does not mean Japanese society has remained totally free of social discrimination. The country's 670,000 Koreans, many of them residents of Japan for two or more generations, regularly protest against their second-class status. The Ainu, an ethnically distinct community regarded by anthropologists as the islands' original settlers and now grouped almost exclusively in Hokkaido, campaign for civil rights in a movement similar to that of Native Americans in the US.

A third group, not of different ethnic origin from the Japanese mainstream but unquestionably inferior in status, are the *burakumin* ("village dwellers," a euphemism for their old caste name—meaning "much filth"— which was officially abolished at the end of the 19th century). They are descendants of outcasts employed to perform the originally taboo—and still disdained —trades of butchery, leatherwork, garbage collection, and the handling of corpses. They live in

As these busy passers-by in Omotesando demonstrate, nobody "strolls" in Tokyo!

separate hamlets or on city outskirts: 400,000 in Tokyo and an estimated 3 million throughout the country. You're most likely to come across them cleaning up garbage in parks and temple grounds, or shining shoes at railway stations. For weeks after the Kobe earthquake in 1995, mounds of garbage lay uncollected despite the quick resumption of other basic services. Why? One of the worst-hit districts was Nada-ku, a burakumin stronghold that suffered a high casualty and death toll.

For centuries the Japanese national spirit (called *yamato damashii),* embodied in its best sense the honor, endurance, and loyalty expected of every good Japanese. The militarist regime of the 1930s blatantly manipulated the concept to prepare the country for war and regional domination and to convince the people of their innate superiority over the enemy.

The subsequent disillusionment has diluted yamato damashii as an ideal in the eyes of today's younger generation. Despite the renowned management methods and worker efficiency that drove the country's spectacular postwar recovery, many wonder whether traditional Japan's collectivist values can appeal to new generations seeking greater individualism and a more prominent role in the running of family, company, and society.

The constant clash between modern and traditional values leads to the numerous fascinating contradictions you will encounter in Japan.

> **In Japan, the family name comes before the given name. Most people won't appreciate your using their given names unless you're a close acquaintance.**

A long history of absorbing outside influences has resulted in a society in which people expect to have a Shinto baptism, a pseudo-Christian wedding (usually held in a hotel "chapel" and officiated by an unordained foreigner in a robe), and a Buddhist funeral. As in centuries past, people go on mass pilgrimages to witness the spring blossoming of the famous cherry trees or the flaming golds, reds, and ochres of the autumn maples.

But they also don't seem to mind when the tranquillity of a Zen temple rock garden is shattered by recorded announcements blaring from loudspeakers parroting the information already contained in the leaflets provided at the ticket office; when heavy-metal pop music loudly emanates from the radio of the middle-aged owner of a corner grocery store; and when parks, gardens, and hallowed temples are ringed by garish souvenir shops whose shelves display both the tastefully understated and the hideously kitsch.

If you think fanatical following accorded baseball suggests that Japanese society is hopelessly Americanized, you should see what happens when a 15-day *sumo* wrestling tournament is held in cities around the country. The centuries-old ceremony and ritual are more than a match for the razzmatazz of the American import. The slow motion instant replay of a pair of 150-kg (330-pound) sumo champions hurling each other across the ring with an *utchari* backward-pivot throw can be sheer poetry in motion.

Businessmen who by day rule their companies can still—despite a recession that has hit the late-night entertainment industry hard—be seen in nightclubs being pampered by fawning hostesses, giggling over countless glasses of whisky or *sake* and singing karaoke versions of Frank Sinatra's "I Did It My Way," only to collapse in a disheveled heap on the last train home. People who might have spent their day controlling precision systems to turn out cars, cameras, or computer chips sit glassy-eyed and transfixed in front of a pachinko pinball machine, doing nothing but watching hundreds of little metal balls going nowhere. Back home, wives who at first seem passive and subservient are formidably powerful mothers and homemakers, driving their children to scholastic success through "examination hell."

Over this amazing cornucopia presides Emperor Akihito. His father, Hirohito, was until 1946 considered a divinity, the living descendant of the gods that created Japan (or ancient Yamato, as it is more evocatively known). The emperor's role today is mainly symbolic, not unlike that of a modern European monarch. But the imperial family remains largely out of sight, never giving an opinion, wholly removed from the daily life of their increasingly beleaguered subjects. This is a far cry from the assertive Emperor Meiji, whose radical social and political policies in the late-19th century launched Japan into the modern era.

So instead of trying to understand Japan—forget the bizarre theories of "Japaneseness"—just open your eyes, your ears, and of course your mind. Savor the delicacy of the cuisine, which, at its

Visions of the future: a Shinkansen (bullet train) speeds in front of an ultramodern glass building in central Tokyo.

finest, is truly a feast for all the senses. Take in the formal beauties of *kabuki* theater, Zen rock gardens, and *ikebana* flower arrangements; struggle to stay awake through an entire *noh* performance. Participate in the graceful tea ceremony or watch the dazzling display of skill in *kendo* (stick fighting), with its impressively fierce battle cries.

Wherever you go, you will have the chance to admire or criticize, to confirm stereotypes or to note exceptions. This book has been specifically designed to guide the curious visitor to the myriad aspects of the "real Japan"—whatever that might be. Japan is a country where the intriguing, the exotic, and the utterly baffling are commonplace, where little can be taken at face value. Yet few people are so warmly welcoming of strangers as the Japanese. Ultimately, visitors who remain open-minded and ready for adventure will be rewarded by unexpected and unforgettable experiences available nowhere else on the planet.

Welcome to Japan!

A BRIEF HISTORY

According to the earliest official accounts, the eighth-century Kojiki ("Record of Ancient Matters") and Nihon-shoki ("Chronicles of Japan"), the islands of Japan were born of a marriage between the god Izanagi and his sister Izanami. They also—but only later—gave birth to the sun, in the form of the goddess Amaterasu, who endowed the Japanese imperial family with its regalia of bronze mirror, iron sword, and jewel. The mirror is kept to this day at the Shinto shrine of Ise-Shima.

Before you dismiss all this as the mere "myth" of Japan's origins, remember that the Japanese continued to trace the imperial dynasty directly back to those deities until Emperor Hirohito in 1946 denounced "the false conception that the emperor is divine." Many followed Japan's best-known novelist Yukio Mishima in deploring this formal break with tradition, and the creation myth has persisted in the popular imagination, side by side with more realistic versions of Japan's origins.

Prehistory and Early Chronicles

As evidenced by bones, weapons, and pottery most recently uncovered by archeologists, the Asian equivalent of Neanderthal Man crossed a now-submerged land bridge from eastern Siberia to what is now Sakhalin Island and northern Japan some 100,000 years ago. These migrants, who later settled throughout the Japanese archipelago, were the ancestors of the present-day Ainu, whose Caucasoid facial and body hair distinguished them from subsequent immigrants from China, Manchuria, Korea, and perhaps the Malay Peninsula. It was the growth and military assertion of the newcomers that drove the "hairy people" (as they were labeled) back north to their present concentration in Hokkaido.

The oldest Stone Age settlements to be discovered (10,000 B.C.) are known as Jomon ("cord pattern"), after the style of their handmade pottery, which was among the earliest to be found anywhere

A stone shrine in Japan's most famous cemetery — Okunoin at Koyasan.

in the world and of rich and imaginative design. Their inhabitants dwelled in sunken pits and lived from hunting, fishing, and the gathering of roots and nuts. It wasn't until the third century B.C. that techniques of rice cultivation (and wheel-made pottery) arrived from Korea, along with irrigation methods that are still in use today.

The scarcity of flatlands suitable for cultivation made it possible for a small aristocratic elite to gain quick control of the food resources. This set the pattern of hierarchic rule that was to prevail right up to the last half of the 19th century (some would claim, in economic terms at least, that it still persists today).

Although there are no reliable accounts of this period, third-century Chinese documents speak of a Japanese priestess-queen, Himiko, ruling over a land of law-abiding people who enjoyed alcohol and were divided into classes distinguished by tattoo marks. Five centuries later, Japan's own *Kojiki* and *Nihon-shoki* chronicles describe the creation of the imperial dynasty in the year 660 B.C.: the first emperor, Jimmu ("Divine Warrior") — great grandson of the

Sun Goddess's grandson—embarked on an expedition of conquest from Kyushu along the Inland Sea coast to the Yamato plain of the Kinki region (near modern-day Nara).

Plausible chronicling, laced with a dose of mythology, begins with the arrival of Korean scribes at the Japanese court around A.D. 400, at a time when Japan also had a military foothold in southern Korea. The state of Yamato, as early Japan was known, was organized into *uji,* or clusters of clans, together with subordinate guilds of farmers, fishermen, hunters, weavers, and potters, all subject to the dominant uji of the imperial family.

Chinese Influences

The Japanese were forced out of the Korean peninsula in the sixth century, but not before the Koreans had bequeathed to the Yamato court copies of the sacred images and scriptures of Chinese Buddhism.

Just as Christianity introduced Mediterranean culture into northern Europe, so Buddhism brought Chinese culture into Japanese society. Throughout the seventh and eighth centuries numerous Japanese monks, scholars, and artists made the perilous trip west across the Sea of Japan to study Chinese religion, history, music, literature, and painting—later to be brought back for further development in Japan.

An outstanding figure of this time was Prince Shotoku, who in 604 developed the "Seventeen-Article Constitution," outlining a code of human conduct and the ideals of state as a basic law for the nation. He also established relations with the Sui dynasty in China. Through him, the Japanese imperial court developed Chinese patterns of centralized government, with its formal bureaucracy of eight court ranks. The Chinese calendar was used to calculate the year of Japan's foundation by counting back the 1,260 years of the Chinese cosmological cycle. Thus, 660 B.C. is still the official date celebrated nationwide.

At this early stage in its history Japan was already (for the most part) only nominally ruled by the emperor. De facto power was exercised by the militarily and economically strongest family. The Sogas

Buddhism — Japanese Style

The spiritual philosophy of Buddhism originated in India around 500 B.C. with the teachings of Siddhartha Gautama, the Indian prince who became the Buddha (Sanskrit for "Enlightened One"). Buddhism soon split into two schools. Theravada, "Doctrine of the Elders," considered closer to the original teachings, is practiced in Sri Lanka, Burma, Thailand, and Cambodia. Mahayana, the "Larger Vehicle," which is comparable in its ritual and social evolution to Christianity, is followed in China, Korea, and Japan.

Pure Buddhist doctrine teaches the quest for enlightenment (nirvana) by the progressive abandonment of desire, which is the source of all life's pain. In Japan, partly because of the language barrier of the scriptures but also because of a general resistance to metaphysical thought, Buddhist practice shifted away from private contemplation to public charity work. The requirements of celibacy and asceticism were also gradually dropped.

For the Japanese, Buddhism initially appealed as a magical protector of both the state and the noble families, who built temples near their homes. New sects in the 9th century spread Buddhism throughout the country. The religion evolved from protector of the aristocracy to vehicle of faith and hope for the common people, who were attracted by the prayers and elaborate rituals.

By the 12th century Buddhism had integrated successfully with the indigenous Shinto religion. It was also suffused with those elements of Chinese Confucianism appropriate to the Japanese character: family solidarity, filial piety, and loyalty to the ruler and to authority in general. As always, the Japanese proved to be not slavish imitators but ingenious adapters.

had promoted Buddhism as an imperially sanctioned counterweight to the native Shinto religion, along with the new Chinese customs, to weaken the influence of their more conservative rivals. But they in turn were ousted in A.D. 645 by Nakatomi Kamatari, founder of the great Fujiwara clan, which was to rule Japanese affairs for hundreds of years and provide prominent advisers to the emperor even up to the 19th century.

The Nara Period

Another of the new ideas was to set up a permanent residential capital for the imperial court, initially at Naniwa (present-day Osaka) and then a little to the east, at Nara, in 710. Laid out like a chessboard (nearly half the size of China's similarly designed capital, Chang'an), Nara had its imperial palace at the northern end, with court residences, Buddhist monasteries, and Shinto shrines stretching to the south. In those peaceful years, without threat of foreign invasion or civil war, there were no city ramparts.

The era known as the Nara Period was marked by the religious fervor of the Buddhist monks and also by their accompanying artistic achievements. The Japanese were attracted more to Buddhism's ritual and art than to its complex philosophy, rendered all the more difficult because its texts were, for several centuries, available only in Chinese, the language of a small court elite. Buddhist monks initiated great progress in Japanese architecture, bronze-casting, bridge-building, and sculpture. To this day, historians of Chinese art find the best surviving examples of Tang-dynasty architecture among the seventh- and eighth-century temples in and around Nara.

By marrying his daughters to sons of the reigning emperor and then engineering timely abdications, a Fujiwara contrived always to be father-in-law, uncle, or grandfather behind the throne. Very often the emperor was only a minor, so that the Fujiwara patriarch acted as regent. He then persuaded the emperor to abdicate soon after his majority, and the regency would continue for the next youthful incumbent. The important thing was to have the emperor's sanction for the regent's political decisions.

Very few emperors were reluctant to submit to Fujiwara domination. The burden of his spiritual functions as high priest of Shinto and the tasks of administration led the emperor to welcome an early abdication, frequently to retire to a life of Buddhist meditation and scholarship. The Fujiwara resented the Buddhist clergy's great and growing influence in imperial affairs. There were too many monasteries in and around Nara. It was time to move the capital.

The Golden Heian Era

The geomancers in 794 decided that Heian-kyo (modern Kyoto) would be an auspicious site for the imperial family. It was indeed— until 1869.

Grants of tax-free land over the years had been made to Buddhist temples and members of the court aristocracy. The most powerful families thus carved out for themselves whole regions that were to become the fiefdoms of Japanese feudalism. By the end of the eighth century the clans had created a hierarchy of *shiki,* or rights, from the highest to the lowest ranks of society. The aristocrat or court patron lent his prestige to a powerful provincial proprietor, who employed a competent estate-manager to oversee smallholders, who in turn worked their farms with dependent laborers. This elaborate structure of interdependent rights and obligations was to serve Japanese society right into the 20th century.

Meanwhile, Heian court life blossomed in an effusion of aesthetic expression. Princes and princesses judged the merits of birds, insects, flowers, roots, or seashells. Literary party games held in ornate palace gardens required each guest to compose a small poem as his wine cup floated toward him along a miniature winding chan-

Relic from the past: a lavishly adorned golden buddha in Nara's Todaiji Temple.

*The tea ceremony is a Japanese tradition that goes back
many centuries.*

nel of water. Expeditions were organized to the best viewing points
for the first spring cherry blossoms, and special pavilions were built
to watch the rising of the full moon. Every gesture, from the most
banal opening of an umbrella to the sublimest act of lovemaking,
had its appropriate ceremonial. Conversation often took the form of
elegant exchanges of improvised verse.

The changing role of Chinese culture in Japanese life was epito-
mized in the language itself. In the absence of an indigenous alpha-
bet, Japanese scholars had with the greatest difficulty tried to adapt
the complex ideograms of monosyllabic Chinese to the essentially
polysyllabic Japanese. Thus developed the *katakana* system used as
a vehicle for writing Buddhist names and concepts.

After rival Fujiwara factions had been struggling for years to gain
control of the imperial throne, they turned to the Taira and
Minamoto armies in 1156 to wage the four-year war that heralded

the end of the golden age of the Heian court. The Taira, controlling the region along the Inland Sea, defeated the Minamoto armies based in the Kanto province east of the capital.

Over the next 20 years, the Minamoto clan acquired new strength by offering better guarantees to local landowners—and their armies—than they could expect from court. Eventually a new offensive, the decisive Gempei War, was launched in 1180. Five years later, the Taira were overthrown after being defeated in the straits between western Honshu and Kyushu, at the titanic sea battle of Dannoura—which has a place in Japanese annals comparable to Waterloo or Stalingrad.

Enter the Shoguns

Japan's austere, ruthless, but statesmanlike new ruler, Yoritomo Minamoto, set up his government in Kamakura (just south of modern Tokyo), well away from the "softening" influence of court life that had been the undoing of his predecessor, Kiyomori. First of the national rulers to take the title of *sei-i tai-shogun* ("barbarian-subduing great general"), Minamoto expanded and consolidated his power by confiscating lands from some of the defeated Taira and redistributing them to his samurai vassals.

Minamoto died in 1199, and the feudal structure passed intact to the tutelage of his widow's family, the Hojo, who were content to play regent to a figurehead shogun, in much the same way as the Fujiwara had done with the emperor. The fiction of Japanese imperial power had become infinitely extendable. The emperor at Kyoto—still seconded by a Fujiwara regent at court—legitimized a Minamoto who was himself a military dictator controlled by a Hojo regent. In a country where form and substance were inextricably interrelated, two things counted in politics: symbolic authority and real power. Neither could exist without the other.

A thwarted Mongol invasion in 1274 weakened the Kamakura regime. The fighting brought none of the usual spoils of war that provincial warlords and samurai had come to expect as payment. And the treasury was empty after earthquake, famine, and plague had crippled the economy. Buddhist monasteries were using their private armies to support imperial ambitions to bring power back to Kyoto. Worst of all, the Kamakura warriors, resenting the way the Kyoto court referred to them as "Eastern barbarians," sought refinement in a ruinous taste for luxury: extravagant feasts, rich costumes, and opulent homes. Kamakura was falling apart.

Creative Turmoil

The subsequent power struggle at first split the country into two imperial courts, and then effective control of Japan was splintered for two centuries among scores of daimyo (feudal warlords).

Eventually, the Ashikaga family shoguns settled down in Kyoto's Muromachi district, which gave its name to the new creative period that followed. The gruff, bluff warriors' taste for art—calligraphy, landscape painting, the tea ceremony, music, dance, and theater— coincided with a renewed interest in things Chinese, above all the teachings of Zen Buddhism. Although Zen had been present in Japan since the 12th century, its ascendancy began under the Kamakura regime, which found the mystic Chinese philosophy admirably suited to Japanese sensitivity, impressionism, and love of form and ritual.

The Ashikaga shoguns and their samurai were greatly attracted by an essentially anti-intellectual doctrine that transmitted its truth from master to disciple by practical example rather than scholarly study of texts. Enlightenment (satori) was to be achieved through self-understanding and self-discipline, combining tranquillity and individualism. After their savage battles, the warriors recuperated through meditation in the peace of a Zen monastery rock garden.

From 1467 to 1568, civil war constantly raged up and down the country among some 260 daimyo, from which a dozen finally emerged victorious. They had fought with mass armies of infantry rather than relying on the old cavalry elite. Although swords, bows,

Interest in landscape painting and other Chinese arts made a resurgence under the Ashikaga shoguns.

and arrows remained the mainstays of warfare, suddenly matchlocks, muskets, and cannons made their appearance. The Europeans had arrived.

In 1543 Portuguese explorers reached Tanegashima Island, off southern Kyushu, followed over the next decade by Portuguese traders and Jesuit missionaries, headed by St Francis Xavier, who landed at Kagoshima in 1549. Many Kyushu daimyo adopted Christianity as a means of winning favor with the Portuguese traders, without necessarily abandoning their Buddhist beliefs or Shinto practices. Converted nine years earlier, daimyo Omura founded the port of Nagasaki as a center for Portuguese trade in 1571. The town was handed over to the Jesuits in 1579. By 1582, Christian converts were estimated at 150,000; by 1615 there were half a million throughout the country. (Through all the vagaries of persecution and war, Nagasaki has remained the major center of Japanese Christianity.)

Trade with the Portuguese — and the Dutch — launched a craze for tobacco, bread, potatoes, clocks, pantaloons, and eyeglasses, the latter very often worn as a chic symbol of intellectual superiority rather than as an aid for poor eyesight.

Momoyama Unification

By 1568, when Kyoto was at last seized from the Ashikaga shogunate, three ruthless generals — Nobunaga, Hideyoshi, and

Tokugawa—had banded together to eliminate all remaining opposition. Realizing the importance of Western military technology, Nobunaga mastered the manufacture of gunpowder and made firearms from melted-down temple bells. The triumphant trio were the first to develop the appropriate defenses against the new firepower. They replaced the old small castles on high ground protected only by wooden stockades with large central fortresses out of

The massive ramparts of Osaka Castle's outer moat, breached by the Tokugawa shogun.

range behind broad moats, surrounded by solid stone ramparts and earthworks strong enough to resist cannon fire.

Cleverest of the three, Nobunaga used another Western weapon, Christianity, against the principal remaining threat to his authority—the strongholds surrounding Kyoto. While sending out armies to destroy the Buddhist monasteries and confiscate their lands, he simultaneously fostered Christianity to win adepts away from the Buddhist faith.

Nobunaga was assassinated by one of his own generals in 1582, and Hideyoshi, who had started out as a simple infantryman, succeeded him. Seeing in Christianity a threat to his central authority, Hideyoshi systematically suppressed Christian activity; in 1597 six missionaries and 20 Japanese converts were crucified at Nagasaki. He was also a master of the art of conspicuous consumption, contrasting sharply with the restraint shown by the Ashikaga shoguns in their more subtle displays of wealth. The gigantic castle he erected at Osaka was the biggest Japan had ever seen, requiring a work force of 30,000 men. Perhaps his most astounding coup was the monstrous Kitano tea ceremony attended by hundreds of rich and poor followers, who were all obliged to stay to the end. It lasted ten days.

A 16th-century warlord once made functional musket barrels from rolled up layers of lacquered Japanese paper. It's that strong.

Tokugawa Takes All

When Hideyoshi died in 1598, he hoped to have his five-year-old son continue his "dynasty," initially under the tutelage of five regents. But one of the regents was Ieyasu Tokugawa, who had been biding his time at Edo for 12 years, nurturing dynastic ambitions of his own. Of the cunning, ruthless triumvirate that came out on top at the end of the country's century of civil war, Tokugawa was without doubt the most patient, the most prudent—and most treacherous. He moved quickly to eliminate his strongest rivals, crushing them in 1600 at the great Battle of Sekigahara (near modern Nagoya).

During its subsequent two and a half centuries of rule from the new capital established at Edo, the Tokugawa organized a tightly controlled coalition of some 260 daimyo in strategic strongholds throughout the country. The allegiance of this highly privileged and prestigious group was ensured by cementing their ethical principles in the code of *bushido,* "the way of the warrior": loyalty to one's master, defense of one's status and honor, and fulfillment of all

The Way of the Gods

The major tenets of Shinto—Japan's indigenous religion—were the imperial family's direct descent from the Sun Goddess and the resulting divinity of the emperor. Although his divinity was renounced only after World War II, the emperor remains Shinto's titular head.

Literally "the way of the gods," Shinto has a strong component of nature worship, with shrines in such places of great natural beauty as mountain tops or forests, where divine spirits are believed to inhabit waterfalls, unusual rocks, or great trees. Followers of Shinto respect the deities through ritual purification ceremonies. Menstruation, childbirth, sickness, injury, and death are all considered sources of impurity—so that workers in slaughterhouses, leather tanneries, or graveyards have traditionally been restricted to a caste of "untouchables," known today as the *burakumin.*

Shinto remains a much less solemn religion than Westerners are used to. The commercial bustle around Tokyo's Asakusa shrine typically evokes the atmosphere of a Western country fair. In front of the shrine, people clap their hands to attract the gods' attention, bow respectfully, toss some coins into a slotted box, and offer up a prayer. Then they go off to the food stalls, amusement booths, and souvenir shops, all located inside the sanctuary grounds. In few countries do religion and commerce coexist so harmoniously.

Hear none, Speak none, See none—monkeys demonstrate their aversion to evil at the Toshogu Shrine at Nikko.

obligations. Loyalty was further enforced by holding the vassals' wives and children hostage in Edo. All roads into Edo, the most famous being the Tokaido Highway, had checkpoints for guns coming in and for wives going out.

One of the most effective ways of keeping a tight rein on the country was to cut it off from the outside world, to keep Japan Japanese. At first, Ieyasu Tokugawa was eager to promote foreign trade. He wanted silk and encouraged the Dutch and British as good, nonproselytizing Protestants just interested in trade. But he didn't like the Portuguese and Spanish Catholic missionaries, who he felt were undermining traditional Japanese values. He banned their activities in 1612 and two years later ordered the expulsion of all missionaries and unrepentant Japanese converts. Executions and torture followed. Converts were forced to renounce their faith by trampling crucifixes and effigies of

Jesus and Mary. The Catholic Church has counted 3,125 martyrs in Japan from 1597 (beginning under Hideyoshi) to 1660.

In 1635 the Japanese were forbidden, on pain of death, to attempt to travel abroad, and Japanese citizens already overseas were prevented from returning, in case they brought back subversive Christian doctrines. Western books were banned, as were Chinese books that mentioned Christianity. After the purge of foreigners, only a few stayed on, strictly confined to Dejima Island in Nagasaki Bay.

This isolation slowed Japan's technological and institutional progress almost to a halt. But it also had the effect of permitting a great, distinctive cultural growth with a strong national identity. The Tokugawa thus celebrated the ancestral religion of Shinto—glorified by the monumentally opulent shrines they built at Nikko. Combining Shinto ritual with official Buddhist conformity, they revived the Confucian ideals of filial piety and obedience to authority to bolster their government.

Commerce thrived, partly in response to the extravagant demands of the Tokugawa court. Merchants thronged to the large cities that were growing up around the castles at Edo (population already 1 million in the 18th century), Osaka (400,000), and Nagoya and Kanazawa (each 100,000)—all huge in comparison with European cities of the time. Japan's overall population in the 18th century was already about 30 million.

Merchants played an active role in creating the urban culture that burgeoned at the end of the 17th century, the so-called Genroku era. Before these hard-working family men went home from work, they liked to drink strong alcohol in the company of actresses and prostitutes. These were the forerunners of the geisha—literally "accomplished person"—with a beauty and refinement that the merchants did not seek in their wives, whom they valued for their childbearing and good housekeeping. These were also halcyon days for the classic *noh* theater, the more popular *kabuki,* and the puppet theater (today's *bunraku)* at Osaka, which was Japan's cultural capital at a time when Edo had more politicians and soldiers than artists.

In the end it was the very rigidity of their unshared control of the country that brought about the downfall of the Tokugawa. Without access to foreign markets, there was no way to counter the rash of catastrophes—plague, drought, floods, and famine—at the end of the 18th century. Uprisings in the towns and countryside began to pose serious threats to the shogun's authority. The Tokugawa reaction was characteristic: a reinforcement of the austere values of the samurai and a rigorous clamp-down on the merchants' high life. There was no more gambling, prostitutes were arrested, and men and women were segregated in the public bathhouses, with naked government spies to enforce the (short-lived) new rules.

Facts and Figures

Area: ranked 42nd in world, with 377,728 square km (147,200 square miles) of surface area on four main islands plus about 3900 smaller islands. Mountains cover 72 percent of the land. Highest point: Mt. Fuji, at 3,776 m (12,388 ft).

Population: ranked 7th in world, with approximately 120 million Japanese, 670,000 Koreans, and 130,000 other non-Japanese residents. Density: 316 per square km.

Capital: Tokyo (metropolitan population 8,330,000).

Major cities: Yokohama (2,900,000), Osaka (2,700,000), Nagoya (2,100,000), Kyoto (1,500,000), Sapporo (1,500,000), Kobe (1,400,000), Fukuoka (1,100,000), Kita-Kyushu (1,100,000), Kawasaki (1,000,000), and Hiroshima (900,000).

Government: Parliamentary democracy, headed by Prime Minister and cabinet, with emperor as titular head of state. Parliament (Diet) comprises House of Representatives (511 seats) and House of Counselors (252 seats). Country divided into 47 prefectures, each with a governor.

The Yankees Are Coming

The feeling began to grow that the only way out of the crisis was to open the country to foreign trade and new ideas. The Tokugawa shoguns, however, sensed that the internal strains might be contained, by sheer brute force if necessary, as long as new pressures were not exerted from outside by foreigners once again offering disgruntled daimyo new sources of income.

The stubborn Americans came back again in 1853, with Commodore Matthew Perry bringing for the shogun (whom he mistook for the emperor) a polite but insistent letter from President Millard Fillmore and a promise to return the next year, with a bigger squadron, for a positive response.

In 1854 Perry duly negotiated the Treaty of Kanagawa (now part of Yokohama), opening up two ports, Shimoda on the Izu Peninsula and Hakodate in Hokkaido. A short time later, similar treaties were signed with Britain and Russia. The West had driven in the thin end of its wedge. More and more ports were opened to foreign trade, and the Japanese were obliged to accept low import tariffs.

As the Tokugawa shoguns had feared, this opening of the floodgates of Western culture after such prolonged isolation had a traumatic effect on Japanese society. The Tokugawa had successfully persuaded the samurai that traditional Japanese values might suffer, and now the samurai felt betrayed, rallying under the slogan "Sonno joi!" ("Honor the emperor, expel the barbarians!").

Before they could even think of accepting contact with the outside world, national integrity had to be restored, under the renewed moral leadership of the emperor. Bands of samurai assassinated British and Dutch representatives. In 1863, the daimyo of Choshu (in western Honshu) fired on foreign ships in the Shimonoseki Straits. In response, the Americans, British, Dutch, and French combined forces to smash the Choshu fortified positions, and Britain retaliated for the assassination by practically leveling the town of

Kagoshima in southern Kyushu. The local daimyo of Satsuma was so impressed that he started to buy British ships, which became the foundation of the future Imperial Japanese Navy.

The Meiji Restoration

In 1868 the Satsuma and Choshu clans, never a real threat to Tokugawa authority as long as they remained rivals, joined forces to overthrow the shogun and restore the authority of the emperor, the 14-year-old Mitsuhito. Edo was renamed Tokyo ("Eastern Capital"), and Mitsuhito took over the Tokugawa castle as his palace.

But important though the resuscitated imperial authority undoubtedly was, the real power under the restoration known as *Meiji* ("Enlightened Rule") was in the hands of a new generation of forward-looking administrators, who set about abolishing the ancient feudal apparatus in favor of a modern government based on merit rather than ancestry. They emphasized the need to acquire Western military and industrial skills and technology with which to confront the West itself and eliminate unfair trade tariffs and other unjust aspects of the foreign treaties.

Agriculture, commerce, and traditional manufacturing were expanded to provide a sound economic base for investment in the modern technology of textiles and other industries. Shipbuilding and weapons manufacture were already under way; railways and telegraph lines quickly followed. And to show just how fast Japan's new rulers were catching on, two punitive expeditions were launched against Korea and China in the grand manner of 19th-century gunboat diplomacy.

There was an inevitable reaction to rapid Westernization. Traditional Japanese theater, the tea ceremony, *ikebana* flower arrangement, and the old martial arts all came back into favor. In 1890 an important imperial edict on education was issued, promoting Asian (that is, Chinese and Japanese) values in culture and stressing loyalty to the emperor and general harmony. If the singing in school of military songs such as "Come, Foes, Come!" or "Though the Enemy Be

Tens of Thousands Strong" seems excessively belligerent today, we should not forget jingoistic attitudes in Europe and America at the time.

Japan made a dramatic debut on the international stage, with military actions against China and Russia. The 1894 Sino-Japanese War for control of the Korean markets and the strategic region of southern Manchuria was a triumph for Japan's modernized army over China's larger but much less well-organized forces. More impressive still was Japan's success against the powerful war machine of Czarist Russia (1904–1905), beginning with a surprise nighttime attack on the Russian fleet, to be repeated some years later at Pearl Harbor. The West was forced to accept Japan's occupation of southern Manchuria and the annexation of Korea in 1910.

A statue of Madame Butterfly points the way through a park in Nagasaki.

In just 40 years, Japan had established itself as a viable world power.

Triumph and Disaster

The 20th century saw a stupendous release of energies that had been pent up for the 250 years of Tokugawa isolation. By 1930 raw-material production had tripled the figure of 1900, manufactured goods had increased twelve-fold, and heavy industry was galloping towards maturity. Britain led the World War I allies in large orders for munitions, while Japan expanded sales of manufactured goods to Asian and other markets cut off from their usual European suppliers. Merchant shipping doubled in size and increased its income ten-fold as the European fleets were destroyed.

Setbacks in the 1930s caused by the European postwar slump were only a spur to redouble efforts by diversifying heavy industry into the machine-making, metallurgical, and chemical sectors. Even the terrible 1923 Tokyo earthquake, which cost over 100,000 lives and billions of dollars, provided another stimulus due to the construction boom that followed.

Riding the crest of this economic upsurge were the *zaibatsu* conglomerates—a dozen family-run combines, each involved in mining, manufacturing, marketing, shipping, and banking. These tightly controlled commercial pyramids were the true heirs to the old feudal structures.

Japan's progress toward parliamentary democracy was halted in the

Japan has its own calendar system, based on the name each new emperor chooses for his reign. The year 2000 is Heisei 12.

1930s by the growing nationalism being imposed on government by the generals and admirals. They proclaimed Japan's mission to bring progress to its backward Asian neighbors in language not so very different from that of the Europeans in Africa or the US in Latin America. After the Russian Revolution of 1917, the Soviet Union was regarded as a major threat to Japan's security, and the army felt it needed Manchuria and whatever other Chinese territory it could control as a buffer against Russian advances. In 1931 the Japanese occupied Manchuria. And then in 1937, with the popular support of ultra-right-wing groups, the army overrode parliamentary resistance in Tokyo and went to war against the Chinese Nationalists. By 1938, they held Nanking, Hankow, and Canton.

Japanese expansionist policies were leading to direct confrontation with the West. Japan hoped that war in Europe would divert the

Soviet Union from interference in East Asia, giving Japan a free hand both in China and, through its alliance with Germany, in French Indochina after the defeat of France. The US responded to the Japanese invasion of Indochina with a trade and fuel embargo, cutting off 90 percent of Japan's supplies. The result was the attack on the American fleet at Pearl Harbor (7 December 1941) and total war.

Early successes in the Philippines, Borneo, Malaya, Singapore, and the Dutch East Indies enabled Japan to establish the so-called Greater East Asia Co-Prosperity Sphere. The "liberation" of these old European colonies created the basis for postwar independence movements proclaiming the Japanese slogan "Asia for the Asians." Despite this, the various occupied populations quickly found themselves suffering harsher and more brutal treatment than they had ever experienced under their former colonial rulers.

The Battle of Midway, in June 1942—destroying Japan's four aircraft carriers and soon thereafter its merchant navy and remaining naval air power—cut Japan off from its empire. In 1944 General Douglas MacArthur was back in the Philippines to direct the island-hopping advance that ended in the massive fire-bombing of Japan's mostly wood-built cities. In an air raid by 130 B29s, Tokyo was devastated and 100,000 of its inhabitants perished. But Japan was reluctant to sue for peace because the Allies were demanding unconditional surrender with no provision for maintaining the highly symbolic role of the emperor, still considered the embodiment of Japan's spirit and divine origins.

Despite US intelligence reports and monitored communications indicating the desperation of large sections of the Japanese government for peace, the Japanese rejection of the Potsdam Declaration calling for Japan's unconditional surrender was the excuse for unleashing the ultimate weapon of the war. On 6 August 1945, a B29 (the *Enola Gay)* dropped an atomic bomb on the city of Hiroshima, inflicting a level of destruction that astonished even the bomb's designers. Three days later another atomic bomb devastated the southern port of Nagasaki.

One of the few structures to survive the Aug 6, 1945 blast: The "A-Bomb" Dome in Hiroshima.

On 8 August the Soviet Union entered the Pacific battlefront and on the next day marched into Manchuria. Five days later the Japanese people heard the voice of Emperor Hirohito, in his first radio broadcast, announcing that "the war situation has developed not necessarily to Japan's advantage." The emperor renounced his divinity, and US forces took formal control of Japan.

Peace and Prosperity

After years of government propaganda predicting the worst atrocities, most Japanese civilians were surprised at the warmth and friendliness of the occupying forces. The postwar period began, however, with millions of displaced people homeless and starving. To counter a perceived communist threat from the Soviet Union, the US quickly set to work reconstructing the economy by transforming Japan's institutions and devising a new pacifist constitution. Article 9 renounced Japan's right to maintain armed forces, although the ambiguous wording was later taken to permit the creation of a "self-defense" force.

The *zaibatsu* conglomerates that had proved so instrumental in boosting Japan's militarism were disbanded, later to re-emerge as the *keiretsu* trading conglomerates that dominated the economy once again. The entire economy received a massive jump-start with the outbreak of the Korean War, with Japan ironically becoming the chief local supplier for an army it had battled so furiously just a few years earlier.

The occupation lasted until 1952, having already planted the seeds for Japan's future stunning economic success. Economic output was back to prewar levels, and British auto companies provided the support needed to get Japan's auto industry back on its feet. Japanese companies then enthusiastically imported any Western technologies they could get their hands on. This included transistor technology—invented in the US but then considered to have only limited applications—for the surreal sum of $25,000. It was Japan that produced the world's first transistor radio. The electronic technology spurt that followed is now legendary.

Parliamentary democracy finally came into its own, albeit with distinctly Japanese characteristics reflecting the dislike of debate and confrontation and the group-oriented preference for maintaining the appearance of harmony at all times. The government, through the powerful Finance Ministry and Ministry of International Trade and Industry, generously supported favored private corporations: first shipping, then cars, then electronics firms basked in the warmth of the government's loving attentions.

Japan overtook Britain economically in 1964. By the end of the decade, Japan's was the third largest economy in the world—less then two decades after the war had left the country in ruins. Prosperity was not without its own problems: pollution caused by "dirty" industries, a high incidence of stomach ulcers (even suicides) among schoolchildren pressured by over-ambitious parents, and the awkward questions of what to do about nuclear energy.

The famous coziness among politicians, bureaucrats, and private companies, together with the strong cultural emphasis on relationship-building and a lack of transparency and accountability, eventually led to corrupt practices of endemic proportions. Breach-of-trust scandals became common. In an increasingly producer-led economy dominated by price-fixing cartels operating with the government's blessing, consumers were left to foot the bill.

The Inevitable Collapse

The start of asset inflation in the 1980s led to the "bubble economy," with anyone owning land becoming richer by the minute. At one point the land value of the Imperial Palace in Tokyo was thought to be worth more than the entire real-estate value of Canada. With astonishing sums of money sloshing around the economy and Japanese products considered world-beaters everywhere, it seemed to the Japanese that the nation had finally achieved its rightful place in the world.

Everyone expected the double-digit growth rates to continue indefinitely. However, crashing real estate prices had a domino effect on the rest of the economy, and in the early 1990s Japan slipped quickly into stagnation and then recession. Seemingly endemic corruption was compounded by a remarkable dearth of political leadership and decisive action. Indeed, in Japan's consensus-based management system, the response of politicians, bureaucrats, and business leaders seemed to be to look the other way and hope bad news would disappear.

The government's gradual and reluctant admission that, despite previous assurances, banks were sitting on staggering—and long-concealed—amounts of unrecoverable loans (originally secured against land values) caused an unprecedented crisis of confidence.

The Tokyo Dome sports arena, a testament to Tokyo's relentless pursuit of technology and the Japanese love for sports.

Growing economic decline brought record corporate bankruptcies and the end of lifetime employment, as companies were forced to improve efficiency in order to survive.

The irony is that although Japan has continually triumphed over externally imposed adversity and upheavals, it seems unable to imple ment effective reforms to its own systems before problems reach crisis proportions. The rote-learning educational system is still failing to help students develop the individual analytical and problem-solving skills required in the information age. Another example is the banking crisis, which grew to globally alarming proportions over an eight-year period before the government even admitted a problem existed.

Despite these formidable challenges, Japan will probably end up confounding the pessimists. It will likely emerge in the 21st centu-ry as a regional leader in more than just economic terms. No matter what the future holds, Japan will remain one of the world's most intriguing destinations for travelers everywhere.

Historical Landmarks

Jomon Culture (ca. 10,000 b.c.–250 b.c.)

Societies live by hunting, fishing, and gathering.

660 b.c.	Legendary founding of first imperial dynasty.

Yayoi Culture (ca. 250 b.c.–a.d. 300)

Techniques of wheel-made pottery and wet rice cultivation arrive from China and Korea.

Yamato Period (ca. 300–710)

ca. 300	Unification of Japan under Yamato Court. Period of Chinese influence.
ca. 538	Introduction of Buddhism from China. Rise to power of Soga family.
645	Soga ousted by Nakatomi Kamatari, founder of Fujiwara dynasty.

Nara Period (710–784)

710	Imperial Court established at Nara.

Heian Period (794–1185)

794	Imperial Court moves to Heian-kyo.
1156	Four-year war between Taira and Minamoto clans.
1185	Battle of Dannoura; Minamoto prevail.

Kamakura Period (1192–1333)

1192	Yoritomo Minamoto becomes first shogun.
1274–81	Unsuccessful Mongol invasions under Kublai Khan.
1333	Fall of Kamakura.

Muromachi Period (1338–1573

1339–1573	Shogunate of Ashikaga family.
1467–1568	Civil war between provincial daimyo.
1543–49	Arrival of Portuguese explorers and Jesuit missionaries.

| 1568 | Rise to power of Nobunaga, Hideyoshi, and Tokugawa. |

Momoyama Period (1573–1600)

1582	Nobunaga assassinated; Hideyoshi succeeds him.
1587	Persecution of Christians begins.
1592	Hideyoshi launches failed attack on Korea and China.
1598	Death of Hideyoshi; Tokugawa seizes power.

Edo Period (1603–1867)

1603	Ieyasu Tokugawa takes title of shogun; capital established at Edo (Tokyo).
1635	Isolation of Japan from rest of world begins.
1854	Treaty of Kanagawa opens Japan to US trade.

Meiji Restoration (1868–1912)

1868	Emperor Meiji comes to throne, restoring imperial power.
1894–95	Sino-Japanese War.
1904–05	Russo-Japanese War.

Modern Period (1912–present)

1937	Japan declares war on Chinese Nationalists.
1940	Japan joins Axis powers in World War II.
1941	Japan bombs Pearl Harbor.
1945	Atom bombs dropped on Hiroshima and Nagasaki; Japan surrenders.
1945–52	US occupation of Japan.
1952–93	Rapid growth and industrialization make Japan the world's second richest nation.
1989	Death of Emperor Hirohito; Akihito succeeds to throne.
1993–99	Japan enters recession, begins to restructure its economy.

WHERE TO GO

To help you plan your itinerary, we divide Japan into seven regional sections. The first is devoted entirely to Tokyo, where you're likely to begin your trip, get your bearings, and become acquainted with modern Japan. We then present six tours spreading out from the capital to the centers of historic and artistic interest as well as to sites of natural beauty. If you have sufficient time to explore Japan, you might want to begin and end your visit in Tokyo. In between, you can venture out to explore the rest of the country.

TOKYO

Originally known as Edo (meaning "estuary"), **Tokyo** was just a sleepy little village surrounded by marshland on the broad Kanto plain until the end of the 16th century, when Tokugawa Ieyasu moved here and made it the center of his vast domains. When Ieyasu became shogun in 1603, Edo in turn became the seat of national government—and its castle the largest in the world. Edo expanded rapidly to accommodate Ieyasu's 80,000 retainers and their families and the myriad common people who served their daily needs. By 1787 the population had grown to 1,368,000.

The ruling elite lived on the high ground, the Yamanote ("bluffs") west and south of the castle. The artisans, tradespeople, and providers of entertainment (reputable and not so reputable) lived "downtown" on the reclaimed marshlands north and east, in the area still known as Shitamachi. As these two populations interacted, a unique new culture was born. Edo became the center of power and also the center of all that was vibrant and compelling in the arts.

After 1868 that center grew even stronger, when the movement known as the Meiji Restoration overthrew the Tokugawa shogunate and the imperial court moved to Edo. The city was renamed Tokyo ("Eastern Capital"), and from that moment on all roads—political, cultural, and financial—led here.

In the 20th century Tokyo has twice suffered almost total destruction. First, the earthquake of 1923 and subsequent fire razed nearly all vestiges of old Edo, killing some 140,000 people in the process. Rebuilt without any comprehensive urban plan, Tokyo remains a city of subcenters and neighborhoods, even villages, each with its own distinct personality.

Unlike the great capital cities of Europe, there is no prevailing style of architecture here, no "monumental" core for a new building to harmonize or clash with. Even after the collapse of the economic bubble in 1992, construction projects are everywhere. Whole blocks of the city seem to disappear overnight, replaced in the blink of an eye by new office buildings, condominiums, cultural complexes, and shopping centers.

Tokyo is a city of enormous creative and entrepreneurial energy, much of which goes into reinventing itself. If there's a commodity in short supply here, it's relaxation. Nobody "strolls" in Tokyo, and there are few places to sit down outdoors and watch the world go by. The idea of a long, leisurely lunch hour is utterly alien. People in Tokyo are in a hurry to get somewhere—even if they don't always know precisely where they're going.

The Imperial Palace

If Tokyo can be said to have any center at all, this is it. Today's **Imperial Palace** is on the site of Edo castle, where the Tokugawa shogunate ruled Japan for 265 years; it was thereafter home to the emperors of the modern era. The palace was almost totally destroyed in the air raids of World War II, then rebuilt in ferroconcrete. This is the least interesting part of what was once the largest system of fortifications in the world, and in any case you can't get in to see it. What you can see are the lovely grounds of the East Garden, the moat and massive stone ramparts, and those few examples of classic Japanese architecture—gates, bridges, armories, and watchtowers —that have survived since the 17th century.

The imperial family still resides in the palace, so the general public is admitted to the grounds on only two days each year, on 2 January and 23 December. On these occasions, you might find it hard to compete with the many thousands of Japanese visitors who come to pay their respects.

The Imperial Palace's **East Garden** is open to the public every day except Monday and Friday. From Otemachi subway station, you enter the gardens at the Otemon Gate and wander through hedgerows of white and pink azaleas, around ponds and little waterfalls edged with pines, plum trees, canary palms, and soft green *cryptomeria japonica*. Over the treetops you catch an occasional glimpse of the skyscrapers of modern Tokyo. Also on the grounds are the **Museum of Imperial Collections**, an exhibition hall for art treasures donated to the public by the imperial family in 1989; and the "Hundred-

Look, but don't enter. One can only view the Imperial Palace from its outer gardens.

Man Guardhouse," where the approach to the inner sanctum of the fortress was defended by four shifts of 100 samurai warriors each.

A walk clockwise around the palace grounds will bring you first to the picturesque **Nijubashi Bridge** and the Seimon Gate, where the public is allowed to enter the palace grounds. You then pass the most prominent of Japan's modern government buildings, the **National Diet** (Japan's parliament) and the **Supreme Court**. A complete circuit would also include the National Theater, and the National Museum of Modern Art. With a short detour, you can also take in **Yasukuni Jinja**. Founded in 1869, this is the "Shrine of Peace for the Nation," dedicated to the souls of those who have died for Japan in battle. Besides the main hall and the hall of worship, the shrine complex includes a *noh* theater stage, a *sumo* wrestling ring, several teahouses, and the Yushukan museum of war memorabilia.

Ginza

Tokyo's best-known district is named after a silver mint originally located here. Once the epitome of chic, **Ginza** has lost many of its smartest young shoppers to the fashion boutiques of districts like Aoyama and Omote-sando, but the area is still fascinating.

The windows of such department stores as Wako and Mitsukoshi are works of art. Inside, there's more art: all the major department stores project themselves as bastions of culture, maintaining their own galleries and mounting frequent world-class exhibitions of prints, painting, pottery, and sculpture. Downstairs you can find still more "art"—to Western eyes at least—in the astonishing basement gourmet food displays. (The basement is also a good place for cheaper snacks than you'll find in the street-level restaurants.)

Running roughly north–south through Ginza from the corner of Hibiya Park all the way to Tokyo Bay is the broad avenue called Harumidori. Taking a stroll down the avenue is such a national institution that there's even a colloquial expression for it: *gin-bura*. Just south of Ginza itself, as you walk toward the bay, you see on your left the red

A Buddhist monk begs for alms at the entrance to the Ginza subway line, located on Tokyo's first underground line.

lanterns and long banners of the **Kabuki-za**, home base for that most thrilling and colorful form of traditional Japanese drama. The first kabuki theater was built in on this site in 1889. Designed to invoke the castle architecture of the Tokugawa period, the theater was destroyed in an air raid in World War II and rebuilt in 1951.

Still farther south is the **Tsukiji Central Wholesale Market**— the largest fish market in Asia. Some 1,600 wholesale dealers do business here, supplying 90 percent of the fish consumed in Tokyo every day. Get here very early (5am is ideal) to see the tuna auctions and enjoy the orchestrated pandemonium of the market at its finest.

From here, you could walk to the lovely Hama Rikyu **Detached Palace Garden**. Originally a Tokugawa family estate, the garden became a public park in 1945. The path to the left as you enter leads to the ferry landing, where the "river buses" depart for their journeys up the Sumida River to Asakusa.

Asakusa

Asakusa is the heart of Shitamachi, the quarter best-beloved of that fractious, gossipy, prodigal population called the Edokko, who trace their "downtown" roots back at least three generations. Edokko are suckers for sentimentality and for *ninjo:* the web of small favors and kindnesses that bind them together. Sneeze in the middle of the night and your Edokko neighbor will demand the next morning that you take better care of yourself; stay home with a fever and she will be over by noon with a bowl of soup. An Edokko craftsman would rather lose a commission than take any guff from a customer who doesn't know good work when he sees it. Edokko quarrel in a language all their own, an earthy local dialect as profane and expressive as Brooklynese. Ignore the proprieties—or offend the pride of an Edokko—

Fresh fish is always available. In fact, Tokyo is home to Tsukiji, Asia's largest fish market.

Other Tokyo Museums

Here are a few of the more interesting public and private museums:

Idemitsu Museum of Arts (Yuraku-cho Station on the Japan Railways Yamanote line). A major collection of Chinese porcelain of the Tang and Song dynasties, and of Japanese ceramics in all the classic Japanese kiln styles. There are also outstanding examples of Zen painting and calligraphy, woodblock prints, and genre paintings of the Edo period.

Bridgestone Museum of Art (Kyobashi subway station). An eclectic private collection of French Impressionist and School of Paris painting, early modern Japanese painting in Western styles, and prints (Rembrandt, Whistler, Manet, Picasso). The collection also includes sculpture from ancient Egypt, classical Greece and Rome, and medieval France.

Japanese Sword Museum (Sangubashi Station on the Odakyu line from Shinjuku). A splendid introduction to the noble and lethal history of Japanese swords—the closest that weapons have ever come to being great works of art.

Mingeikan: Japan Folk Arts Museum (Komaba Todai-mae Station on the Inokashita line from Shibuya). Excellent examples of ceramics, lacquerware, woodcraft, and textiles. It gives a particularly good insight into Japanese furniture that you might not obtain in a private home.

Nezu Institute of Fine Arts (Omote-sando Station on the Ginza subway line). Outstanding works of Japanese painting, calligraphy, and ceramics—including some designated as National Treasures. Equally fine is the collection of ancient Chinese bronze utensils and sculpture. Finer yet, perhaps, is the Institute's wonderful garden: an exquisite composition of pines and flowering shrubs, ponds and waterfalls, moss-covered stone lanterns and tea pavilions.

"Bathing" in the smoke of the Sensoji incense burner is an observance believed to bestow a year's worth of good luck.

and he will let you know about it, in no uncertain terms; respect his sense of values and you make a friend for life.

The heart of Asakusa, in turn, is **Sensoji** (also known as the **Asakusa Kannon temple**). According to legend, the temple houses a small statue of the Buddhist goddess of mercy, found in the Sumida River by two local fishermen in the year 628 — but in fact not even the temple priests have ever seen it. When Edo became the capital of the Tokugawa shogunate, Asakusa began to flourish as an entertainment quarter. In the early-19th century even the kabuki theaters were located here. The Meiji Restoration and the opening of Japan to exotic new Western-style amusements further enhanced Asakusa's reputation as Fun City. The first place in Japan to call itself a "bar" opened in Asakusa in 1880 (and is still doing business); the first movie theater opened here in 1903. Before long, the streets and alleys around the temple were filled with music halls, burlesque theaters, cabarets, gambling dens, and watering holes of every description.

Most of the temple quarter was firebombed to ashes in 1945, but by 1958 the people of the area had raised enough money to rebuild Sensoji and all of the important structures around it. So what if the restorations were in concrete? The original is still there in spirit — and no visitor should neglect it.

Sensoji Temple and Surroundings

Start your exploration from Asakusa Station, on the Ginza subway line (Tokyo's first subway). A few steps from the exit is **Kaminari-mon ("Thunder God Gate")**, the main entrance to the temple, hung with a pair of enormous red paper lanterns. From here, the long, narrow arcade called Nakamise-dori is lined with shops selling toasted rice crackers, spices in gourd-shaped wooden bottles, dolls, toys, fans, children's kimono, and ornaments and souvenirs of all sorts.

> Hold on to your subway and train tickets. They are collected at the turnstile when you reach your destination.

Some of these shops have been operated by the same families for hundreds of years.

The arcade ends at a two-story gate called the Hozomon. To the left is the Five-Story Pagoda, and across the courtyard is the main hall of Sensoji. Visitors should be sure to stop at the huge bronze incense burner in front of the hall, to "bathe" in the smoke — an observance believed to bestow a year's worth of good health.

The building to the right of the main hall is the **Asakusa Jinja**, a Shinto shrine dedicated to the three legendary founders — the Sanja — of Sensoji. (Buddhism and Shinto get along quite peacefully in

Japan, sharing ground and even deities.) The Sanja Matsuri, held here every year on the third weekend in May, is the biggest, most exuberant festival in Tokyo.

Ueno

North of the city center, **Ueno** was chosen in 1625 by the Tokugawa Shogun Hidetaka as the site of a vast temple complex. Called **Kan'eiji**, it was established on the area's one prominent hill to protect the capital from evil spirits. Kan'eiji was a seat of great power until 1868, when it became the battleground in the shogunate's last stand against the imperial army and most of the buildings were destroyed. Subsequently, Ueno was turned into Tokyo's first public park, endowed with all the preferred Western improvements: museums, concert halls, a library, a university of fine arts, and a zoo. Ueno should be a stop on any visitor's itinerary—especially if you happen to be here in mid-April, when the cherry blossoms in the park are glorious.

No visitor here should miss the **Tokyo National Museum**, a complex of four buildings devoted to Japanese art and archaeology dating back to the prehistoric Jomon and Yayoi periods. Outstanding among the exhibits are Buddhist sculpture of the tenth- and 11th-century Heian era, illustrated narrative scrolls from the 13th-century Kamakura period, paintings by the great Muromachi artist Sesshu, and woodblock prints by the Edo-period masters Utamaro, Hiroshige, and Hokusai.

Nor should you neglect the **National Museum of Western Art**, on the east side of Ueno Park: an outstanding collection of French Impressionist paintings, prints, and drawings, the gift of a wealthy businessman named Kojiro Matsukata. The building itself was designed by Le Corbusier; the Rodin sculptures in the courtyard—the *Gate of Hell,* the *Thinker,* and the magnificent *Burghers of Calais*— are authentic castings from the original molds.

Of the Edo-era buildings that have survived or been restored, the most important are the main hall of Kan'eiji and the **Toshogu**

Shoji paper screens in delicate wood frames accentuate the serene, ordered beauty of this tatami mat room.

Shrine to the first Tokugawa Shogun Ieyasu—a lesser version of the great sanctum at Nikko, in the mountains of Nagano Prefecture (see page 64). Also of interest is the **Kiyomizu Kannon Hall**, modeled after the larger and more famous Kiyomizu temple in Kyoto; registered as a National Treasure, this is one of the few buildings that survived the battle of 1868 intact.

At the south end of the park is the statue of Saigo Takamori, leader of the imperial army that overthrew the shogunate in 1868. (Saigo is a problematic hero in Japanese history: in 1871 he was killed in an unsuccessful rebellion against the very government he helped to found.)

From here, it's a short walk west to the grounds of Shinobazu Pond. Just inside the entrance, on the right, is the **Shitamachi Customs and Manners Museum**. Budget some time here: it will give you a wonderfully concrete sense of the lifestyle that defined this part of the city for well over 300 years. The displays include a full-

A local rock group keeps the teens on their feet in the Harajuku district.

scale reproduction of a *nagaya* (one of the long, single-story row houses typical of the Edo period). Visitors are welcome to take their shoes off and walk through the *tatami*-mat rooms.

Harajuku and Yoyogi Park

The venerable imperial traditions of Japan and the frenetic celebration of its youth culture are arrayed side by side in this quarter of the city. From Harajuku Station on the Japan Railways Yamanote loop line, it's but a few steps to **Meiji Jingu**, the shrine dedicated to the spirits of the Emperor Meiji (who died in 1912) and the Empress Shoken. The entrance is marked by two huge *torii* gates, their pillars made from 1,700-year-old cypress trees.

From here, broad gravel paths lead to the *honden* (the sanctum of the shrine), destroyed in the air raids of 1945 and restored in 1958, and the **Imperial Treasure House** museum. The Meiji emperor presided over the emergence of Japan as a modern nation state, and his shrine is surely the most solemn, decorous place in Tokyo. During the annual festival (31 October through 3 November) and on New Year's Day, as many as a million people will come to offer prayers and pay their respects. Spring and summer make better visits, when you can admire the irises and flowering shrubs of the inner gardens.

Adjacent to the shrine is **Yoyogi Park**. The park is remarkable chiefly for the National Yoyogi Sports Center, comprising two stadiums designed by architect Tange Kenzo. The park itself was once a parade ground for the imperial Japanese army. After World War II it was taken over by the Occupation for military housing and nicknamed "Washington Heights," then redeveloped as the Olympic Village site for the 1964 Tokyo Olympic Games. By the 1980s, thanks to the broad avenues and new subway stops built for the games, this had become one of the liveliest, trendiest, and demographically youngest quarters of the city.

On Sundays and holidays, part of the avenue through the park is closed to traffic. Rock bands that are not quite yet on a professional footing truck in their equipment and play all day, just for practice. The bands are loud—they have to be to compete with the groups of Elvis imitators in black leather jackets and sideburns who also lay claim to some of this great free space, dancing in circles to the oldies on enormous boomboxes. Street food, body paint, in-your-face fashion, photo ops: on a warm spring afternoon Yoyogi Park is more fun than any place in town.

The opposite (west) end of the park borders on Shibuya, where you can visit **NHK Broadcasting Center**, headquarters for Japan's public television network—a must for anyone wishing to see how samurai epics are made. Your hotel or the Tourist Information Center will have information on the "Studio Park" guided tour of the NHK soundstages.

Shinjuku

In the Edo period **Shinjuku** was where two of the major roads from the west came together. By the early 1900s the area had become a sort of bohemian quarter, beloved of the city's cliques of writers, artists, and intellectuals. After World War II it emerged as one of Tokyo's major transportation hubs, and today an estimated three million people pass through Shinjuku Station every day. The station itself divides Shinjuku into two distinctly different areas, east and west.

West Shinjuku rejoices in a special gift of nature. Its relatively stable bedrock can support earthquake-safe skyscrapers— foremost among them is the new Metropolitan Government Office, more familiarly known as **Tokyo City Hall**. The City Hall complex was architect Tange Kenzo's magnum opus, arguably the last great work of his career. It was a staggeringly expensive project, and taxpayers have had an ongoing love-hate relationship with its postmodern monumental design since it was completed in 1991. The complex

An estimated three million people pass through Shinjuku station every day.

consists of a 48-story main office building, a 34-story annex, the Metropolitan Assembly building, and a huge central courtyard. The main building soars 243 m (797 ft), splitting on the 33rd floor into two towers. Weather permitting, the observation decks on the 45th floors of both towers offer views all the way to Mt. Fuji

East Shinjuku is really two places: a daytime quarter of department stores, vertical malls, and discount stores, and a nighttime quarter of

Landscaped Japanese gardens offer pockets of tranquility in the hectic city.

bars (straight and gay), cheap restaurants, strip joints, game parlors, jazz clubs, rooms-by-the-hour hotels, raves, and honky-tonks—most of the latter in a seedy, neon-lit neighborhood called **Kabuki-cho**. The neighborhood isn't really dangerous, but it's all too easy for the unwary visitor to wander into a rip-off; if you plan to explore Kabuki-cho, do so with a knowledgeable local guide.

A longish walk along Shinjuku-dori from the station will bring you to the north end of **Shinjuku Gyoen National Garden**. Originally a feudal estate, this collection of gardens (in Japanese, French, and English styles) became part of the imperial household after the Meiji Restoration and, in 1949, a public park—the ultimate oasis in this quarter of the city. Shinjuku Gyoen is famous for its botanical greenhouse, for its flowering cherry trees in April, and for its chrysanthemum exhibition during the first two weeks of October.

Little Buds but Big Obsession

Nightly news bulletins track the progress of the "front" moving across the country at some unpredictable time in April or May. Anticipation reaches fever pitch as people everywhere prepare to make pilgrimages to their favorite vantage points around the country. Yes, it's cherry blossom season once again.

The tradition of formal blossom appreciation and viewing goes back centuries. In Kyoto and Nara, for instance, special viewing pavilions were built for the aristocracy specifically for this purpose. Today, Maruyama Park in Kyoto's Gion district is where numerous drinking parties are held under the blossoms in a cathartic mass-shedding of the usual Japanese reserve. And the grounds of the Osaka Mint heave with citizens trying to catch a glimpse of what is reputedly among the finest examples of the nation's most cherished and celebrated asset.

Over 150 varieties exist, varying in terms of size, color, and exact blooming time. Why the big fuss over these precious pink petals? For many Japanese, the cherry blossom epitomizes the fleeting nature of beauty and purity, the concepts of transience and impermanence that imbue so many aspects of Japanese culture, psyche, and even identity. During World War II, Japan's notorious kamikaze suicide pilots were even romanticized as human cherry blossoms, their young lives abruptly ending after a supposedly dazzling moment of glory.

Shinagawa

 Not otherwise rich in tourist attractions, Shinagawa has one gem that should not be missed: **Sengakuji**—a temple that evokes what is surely the most popular story in all of premodern Japanese history.

In 1701 a young provincial baron named Asano Takumi no Kami, morally insulted by a court official named Kira, attacked and wounded his tormentor. Asano was ordered to commit suicide for his offense; however, Kira went free. Asano's clan steward, Oishi Kuranosuke, and forty-seven of his loyal retainers vowed revenge. On the night of 14 December 1702, despite many obstacles, they attacked Kira's heavily guarded villa on the east side of the Sumida River, cut off his head, and brought it in triumph to Asano's tomb at Sengakuji, the family temple. This was a dilemma for the Tokugawa government. On one hand, their revenge was perfectly in accord with the samurai code of honor; on the other, they had murdered a high official. Eventually, Oishi and his band were also ordered to commit suicide; this they did, and they were buried at Sengakuji with their lord. Celebrated in kabuki theater, film, and television, the story has had an abiding hold on the imagination of the Japanese people. Thousands of visitors come annually to Sengakuji to lay incense on the tombstones and walk through the small museum called the Hall of the Loyal Retainers, where weapons, personal effects, and other memorabilia are preserved.

KANTO

The once-marshy plain of **Kanto** is Tokyo's hinterland, the region where the feudal warlords set up their military bases and administrative headquarters. Their tough-minded pragmatism survives today not only in Tokyo but also in the dynamic industrial zone that has burgeoned around it in such towns as Kawasaki and Yokohama. But monuments at Kamakura and Nikko still bear testimony to the region's history. And reigning supreme over Kanto is a sublime spiritual comment on the vanity of all such human endeavors: sacred Mt. Fuji.

Four easy-to-manage excursions from Tokyo would make memorable additions to your stay. Two of them—to Yokohama and Kamakura—are daytrips. Visits to Nikko and to Mt. Fuji/Hakone will be more enjoyable as overnighters.

Nikko

"Think nothing splendid," says an old Japanese proverb, "until you've seen Nikko." In the mountains of Tochigi Prefecture, about 150 km (93 miles) north of Tokyo by train, **Nikko** is the final resting place of Ieyasu, founder of the Tokugawa shogunate, who died in 1616. Upon his death he was declared a god by the imperial court and subsequently known as Tosho Daigongen ("The Great Incarnation Who Illuminates the East"). The following year, his remains were taken in a grand procession to be enshrined here, on the site of a religious center founded some eight centuries before. In life, Ieyasu had made himself the absolute monarch of Japan. His personal fief alone was worth enough to feed and support some 2.1 million people. **Toshogu**, the mausoleum complex that he commanded for himself in his apotheosis, is extraordinary.

Nikko is best reached from Tokyo by train (by the Japan Railways Shinkansen line from Tokyo or Ueno stations, with a transfer at Utsunomiya, or by the private Tobu Line "Limited Express" from Asakusa). The journey takes about two hours. The little town of Nikko is essentially one long avenue from the railway station to the Toshogu shrine.

The Toshogu Shrine Complex

A short bus ride from the station plaza brings you to the red-lacquer **Shinkyo** ("Sacred Bridge"), a 28-m (92-ft) span over the Daiya River, where your exploration of Toshogu begins. The bridge marks the spot where the Buddhist priest Shodo is said to have crossed the river in the year 766 on the backs of two huge serpents, to found the temple that would later become Rinnoji. An entrance to the shrine complex is just across the road, opposite the bridge and up a flight of stone steps that brings you first to Shodo's temple.

Rinnoji belongs to the Tendai sect of Buddhism. The main hall, called the Sanbutsudo, with its almost erotic color scheme of black and green and vermilion, dates to 1648 and is the largest single building at Toshogu. Inside are three huge gold-lacquered statues, representing three different manifestations of the Buddha. In the center is Amida Nyorai, the Buddha who leads believers to Paradise; on the right is Senju ("Thousand-Armed") Kannon, the goddess of mercy; on the left is Bato-Kannon, depicted with a horse's head on its forehead, regarded as the protector of animals. North of the main hall is the Goho-tendo, a subtemple where worshippers inscribe their prayers for health and prosperity on slats of wood that are later burned to carry the prayers to heaven. To the south is the residence of the Abbot—by tradition an imperial prince—with a particularly fine garden in the style of the Edo period.

Leaving Rinnoji from the west side, you come to the broad Omotesando avenue that leads uphill to the shrine itself. Note the monument to the daimyo Matsudaira Masatane, Ieyasu's trusted retainer. Matsudaira spent some 20 years planting the majestic cryptomeria cedars on the grounds of the shrine and along the 64-km (40-mile) avenue of approach. Alas, much of the avenue has been destroyed; a few sections of it survive on the road east of town, where many of the 13,000 trees still standing are maintained by corporate sponsors.

At the top of the Omote-sando, on the left, is the five-story pagoda of the shrine, decorated with the 12 signs of the Asian zodiac and the hollyhock crest of the Tokugawa family. From here, a flight of stone steps leads to the first gate of Toshogu: the Omotemon, guarded by two fierce red-painted Deva kings. In the first courtyard is the stable, which houses the shrine's sacred white horse; the carved panel above the door is the famous group of three monkeys—"Hear

National treasures—the numerous buildings of the Toshogu Shrine feature a lavish opulence that is found nowhere else in Japan.

no evil, see no evil, speak no evil!"—that has become a symbol of Nikko, the logo on virtually every souvenir. At the far end of the courtyard is the Kyozo (Sutra Library), which houses some 7,000 Buddhist scriptures in a huge revolving bookcase.

As you approach a second set of stone steps, you see on the right a belfry and a tall bronze candelabrum; on the left is a drum tower and a bronze revolving lantern. The two bronzes were presented in the mid-17th century by the Dutch government, in gratitude for the special exemption that gave them exclusive trading privileges with Japan during the period of national seclusion. Off to the left is the Yakushi-do, a temple honoring the manifestation of the Buddha as healer of illnesses.

At the top of the steps is the two-story **Yomeimon**, the "Gate of Sunlight"—the triumphal masterpiece of Toshogu, rightly declared a National Treasure. This is the ultimate expression of the opulent Momoyama style inspired by Chinese Ming sculpture and architecture. Ivory-white and 11.3 m (37 ft) high, its columns, beams, and cornices are carved with a menagerie of dragons, phoenixes, lions, and tigers in a field of clouds, peonies, Chinese sages, and angels, all gilded and painted in red, gold, blue, and green. To the right and left of the gate there are paneled galleries, also carved and painted with a motifs from nature: pine and plum trees, birds of the field, and waterfowl.

Inside the gate to the left is the Mikoshi-gura, a storeroom for the portable shrines that grace the semi-annual Toshogu Festival processions (18 May and 17 October). To the right is the Kaguraden, a hall where ceremonial dances are performed to honor the gods—and where, for a modest fee, couples can have Shinto wedding ceremonies performed, complete with flutes and drums and shrine maidens to attend them.

Opposite the Yomeimon, across the courtyard, is the **Karamon** ("Chinese Gate"), the official entrance to the inner shrine. This structure, like Yomeimon, is also a National Treasure and just as ornately carved and painted. The walls on both sides of this gate enclose the *honden* (main hall) of the shrine.

The entrance is to the right. Here you remove your shoes (lockers are provided) to visit the outer part of the hall, called the *haiden* (oratory). You may not proceed further than this, for at the far end of the oratory are the *naijin* (inner chamber) and *nai-naijin* (innermost chamber), where the spirit of Ieyasu is enshrined. With him are two other worthy companions: Toyotomi Hideyoshi, Ieyasu's mentor, and the great 12th-century warrior Minamoto no Yoritomo, who founded the Kamakura shogunate—and whom Ieyasu claimed as an ancestor.

The tour next takes you to another Toshogu icon: the famous **Gate of the Sleeping Cat**. The cat itself, on a small panel above the entrance, is said to have been sculpted by Hidari Jingoro, a legendary master carver of the Tokugawa period. From here a flight of 207 stone steps takes you up through a wonderful forest of cedars to **Ieyasu Tokugawa's tomb**. The climb is worth making, if only for the view, the trees, and a cool, rushing stream. The tomb itself, a miniature bronze pagoda that houses the great shogun's ashes, is nothing special.

A short walk west from Toshogu itself is surely the oldest of the institutions on this holy ground. **Futarasan Jinja** is a Shinto shrine founded in the 8th century to honor the deity Okuni-nushi-no-Mikoto ("God of the Ricefields"), his consort, and their son. In one corner of the enclosure is a bronze lantern some 2.3 m (7.5 ft) high; the deep nicks in the bronze were made by guards on duty at the shrine, who believed that the lantern transformed itself into a goblin at night. Such was the incredible cutting power of the Japanese sword —embellished perhaps a bit by Japanese superstition.

Iemitsu, who was Ieyasu's grandson and the third Tokugawa shogun (1603–1651), undertook the building of Toshogu. He has his own resting place here at **Daiyu-in**, to the west of Futarasan. Smaller in scale, Daiyu-in is in fact the more impressive mausoleum, set on a forested hillside and approached by three flights of stone stairs and five decorative gates. The most impressive of these, at the top of the stairs, is the Yashamon ("She-Demon Gate"), so named for the figures in its four alcoves. The sanctum of the shrine, designated a National Treasure, has a gilded and lacquered altar some 3 m (nearly 10 ft) high, where a seated wooden figure of Iemitsu looks down upon his mighty works.

Lake Chuzenji

The waterfalls and forested hills of the **Nikko National Park** area are a welcome respite to the monumentality of Tokugawa architecture. Even if you are here only on a daytrip, you should take the 10-km (6.2-mile) bus ride up the spectacular winding Irohazaka Highway to Chuzenji. Better yet, take a cab and tell the driver to stop at Akechi-daira, the halfway point. The view of Mt. Nantai (2,484 m; 8,148 ft) and the valley below is magnificent.

Reaching Out to Touch

Westernization in Japan is much more than simply breathing new life into governmental and industrial practices. In daily life, for example, businessmen often shake hands not as an alternative but as a supplement to the good old-fashioned bow. The handshake seems to complement the respectful formality of a bow with something more satisfyingly personal and sincere, breaching the distance with distinctly un-Japanese physical contact.

Many visitors, though, are uncomfortable with the idea of bowing, since it has strong cultural associations with servility and inferiority. This is natural. But—like everything else in Japan—the significance of the bow needs to be taken in context. Bows are usually not given but exchanged. In a rigidly hierarchical society, the idea is mainly to convey mutual respect and only incidentally to acknowledge one's status relative to another.

If you're still uncomfortable, think of it as a handshake using the entire body. When you meet most Japanese people, they'll be expecting to grip your hand. Even the most token bow you give will pleasantly surprise them.

Lake Chuzenji, at 1,270 m (4,166 ft) above sea level, was made eons ago when a now-dormant volcano erupted and blocked the river courses, creating two cataracts. The 96-m (315-ft) **Kegon-no-taki** at the south end is the country's most famous waterfall. An elevator takes sightseers to an observation platform in the gorge below. The falls are especially impressive after a summer rain, when the sunshine produces a single or even double rainbow in the spray. In the winter the falls form a spectacular cascade of icicles. At the gorge's north end, Ryuzu-no-taki ("Dragon's Head Falls") is broader but not as high; it has the additional merit of a teahouse, where you can sit and watch the water tumble into the lake.

Famous for its rainbow trout, Chuzenji is too cold for swimming most of the year, but visitors throng to this area for its spectacular spring and fall scenery and for its numerous hot springs resorts. The most impressive historical monument on the eastern shore of the lake is Chuzenji, a subtemple of Toshogu's Rinnoji. The temple enshrines a 5 m (16 ft) standing figure of Kannon, the Goddess of Mercy, said to have been carved more than 1,000 years ago from the trunk of a single Judas tree.

Yokohama

Situated 20 km (12.5 miles) southwest of Tokyo, **Yokohama** was an unimportant little fishing village until 1854, when Japan's long centuries of self-imposed isolation came to an end. Foreign diplomats, traders, and missionaries were at last able to enter the country. But the unrest they inspired prompted the Tokugawa government to move them all here, to a guarded compound on the village flats—ostensibly to guarantee their safety, but more importantly to contain the contamination of their uncouth ways and ideas.

The ploy worked well enough until the Meiji Restoration, when those Western ideas were needed to modernize the country. In 1869 Yokohama became an international port, and the burgeoning international community quickly spread beyond its confinement to the

high ground still known today as the Bluff. In 1872 Japan's first railway went into service between Yokohama and Tokyo, and the city began to flourish.

The two cities have twice shared the same destructive fate. The great Kanto earthquake of 1923 destroyed some 60,000 homes in Yokohama and took over 20,000 lives. The next twenty years of reconstruction and growth were wiped out overnight, in May 1945, when American bombers leveled nearly half the city. The harbor was hastily restored during the Korean War and today is one of the busiest and most important trading ports in the world.

With a population of some three million, Yokohama no longer sits in Tokyo's shadow. In many respects, in fact, it is the more cosmopolitan city, preferred by many residents of the greater metropolitan area as a place to live and work. If you are on a short visit to Japan, your excursion time might be better spent elsewhere. But Yokohama's great waterfront, port redevelopment project, museums, and restaurants should still keep it high on your list.

The Japan Railways Keihin-Tohoku line takes about 40 minutes from Tokyo to Sakuragi-cho Station in Yokohama; the faster *shinkansen* leaves you off at Shin-Yokohama, on the outskirts of the city. From Sakuragi-cho it's a short walk to the waterfront (which is still referred to by its old name, the Bund) and to the South Pier and Yamashita Park. Here you can take a tour of the harbor on one of the sightseeing launches moored near the ship *Hikawa-maru,* now retired from service. It carried passengers between Yokohama and Seattle for some thirty years; in summer, it has a pleasant beer garden on the upper deck.

At the entrance to the South Pier is the nine-story Silk Center Building. The **Silk Museum** on the second floor, with its collection of kimono and exhibits of the silk-making process, evokes the period

Also known as the "Swan of the Pacific," the Nippon Maru now resides gracefully in Yokohama harbor.

when Yokohama was the hub of that industry. On the first floor are the main offices of the Yokohama International Tourist Association.

For a bird's-eye view of the harbor, take the elevator to the observation deck of the 106-m (348-ft) **Marine Tower**. The beacon atop the tower gives it a claim of being the tallest lighthouse in the world; it also has an interesting oceanographic museum.

The Minato Mirai 21 project, launched in the mid-1980s, was intended to turn a huge tract of neglected waterfront north and east of Sakuragi-cho into a model "city of the future," integrating business, exhibition, and leisure facilities. The centerpiece of the project is the 70-story **Landmark Tower**, Yokohama's tallest building; its observation deck affords a spectacular view of the city and the Bay Bridge, especially at night.

Nearby is the **Yokohama Museum of Art**, designed by Tange Kenzo and housing works by both Western and Japanese artists, including Picasso, Braque, Kandinsky, Kishida Ryusei, and Yokoyama Taikan. On the waterfront itself is **Nippon-maru Memorial Park**, where pride of place goes to the three-masted sailing ship popularly called the "Swan of the Pacific." Now a training vessel, it is open to visitors on guided tours.

Yokohama's Chinatown, a few minutes' walk from Japan Railways'·Kannai Station in the center of the city, is the largest in Japan. Its narrow alleys are crowded with shops selling foodstuffs, spices, herbal medicines, cookware—in fact, anything that China exports. The restaurants, needless to say, are wonderful.

Fashionable, upbeat Yokohama is centered in two areas. One is Basha-michi ("Horse-Carriage Street") running from Kannai Station to the waterfront. The street acquired its name in the 19th century, when it was laid out for the vehicles of the city's Western residents; a more recent redesign evokes that era with red brick sidewalks and imitation gas lamps—but the boutiques along the street are up-to-the-minute. The other area extends from Ishikawa-cho Station to Motomachi and the International Cemetery. Motomachi was the first

Gateway to Yokohama's Chinatown — the largest such district in Japan, it also marks the center of the city.

area developed in the Meiji period to serve Western shoppers, and it has kept pace with the movements of fashion ever since.

The **International Cemetery**, established in 1854, is the last resting place of some 4,000 foreigners of 40 different nationalities who lived and died in Yokohama. Behind it is the Yamate Shiryokan, a small museum of materials about the city's 19th-century European population. Just up the hill at this end of Motomachi is Harbor View

Park, where the views at night—when Yamashita Park and the harbor are floodlit—are especially fine.

The last must-see in Yokohama is **Sankei-en**, originally the estate of wealthy silk merchant and art connoisseur Hara Tomitaro, who opened his garden to the public in 1906. At great expense he transferred here a number of important 17th-century buildings that once belonged to the Tokugawa family, including the Rinshunkaku villa and the charming Choshukaku tea pavilion, as well as a small temple from Kyoto's famed Daitokuji. Sankei-en is a special delight from February though early April, when the plum and cherry trees blossom.

Kamakura

Kamakura, less than an hour south of Tokyo by train, was the seat of Japan's first military government. The Kamakura shogunate was founded late in the 12th century after a long and bloody rivalry between two noble factions over control of the imperial court. The victorious Minamoto clan chose **Kamakura** as its headquarters because this fishing village—girded on three sides by steep wooded hills—was a natural fortress. Here they created what most of us envision as the "Way of the Samurai": the values, codes, religion, and culture of a warrior caste that would rule Japan for 700 years.

Much of that culture was inspired by the Rinzai sect of Zen Buddhism and its sense of discipline and self-control, its austere philosophy of art and life. The shogunate founded great numbers of Zen temples in Kamakura. Many are still standing, and some are registered as National Treasures. From the Japan Railways station at Kita (North) Kamakura, about an hour from Tokyo on the Yokosuka line, you can easily reach six of these temples.

Engakuji, founded in 1282, became the second most important in the group of monasteries called the Gozan ("Five Mountains"), a hier-

A hike through one of Kamakura's bamboo glades. These wooded hills provided a natural fortress for Minamoto headquarters.

archy established in the 14th century for the Zen temples under the official patronage of the shogunate. Engakuji is Kamakura's largest temple complex; often wracked by fire and earthquake, 17 of the original 46 buildings have survived. Two of these are registered as National Treasures: the *shariden* (hall of holy relics), built in 1282, and the huge belfry on the hill above. The bell, some 2.5 m (8 ft) tall, was cast in 1301. The principle building open to the public at Engakuji is the *butsunichian* ceremonial hall, where visitors can take part in a tea ceremony.

Nearby is **Tokeiji**, familiarly known as the "Divorce Temple," which was unique as a sanctuary for the women of the warrior caste seeking an escape from unhappy marriages. If the victim managed to make her way here and stay for three years as a nun, she could obtain a decree of divorce from the shogunate and go free. The *homotsukan* (treasure house) of Tokeiji has a collection of Kamakura-period paintings, sculpture, and calligraphy, some of which are registered as Important Cultural Objects. Also on the grounds is the Matsugaoka Bunko, a research library established in memory of D.T. Suzuki (1870–1966), who pioneered the study of Zen Buddhism in the West.

South of Tokeiji, on the way to Kamakura's center, are Meigetsu-in and Jochiji, Zen temples with especially fine gardens. Still farther south is **Kenchoji**, founded in 1249, the foremost of the "Five Mountains." It was modeled on one of the great Chinese monasteries of the time and built for a Chinese monk who was said to have interceded with the dreaded Kublai Khan to stop the Mongol invasion of Japan. Kenchoji is still an active monastery; like many of the temples in Kamakura, it offers visitors the opportunity to take part in Zen meditation training sessions. Nearby Ennoji boasts a remarkable group of sculptures representing Enma (the Lord of Hell) and his judges.

Sightseeing in Kamakura

In Kamakura proper, don't miss **Tsuru-ga-oka Hachimangu**, the shrine complex built by Yoritomo no Minamoto, the first Kamakura shogun. It was dedicated to the legendary Emperor Ojin, from whom

Photo op—the stone bridge near the Hachimangu Shrine in Kamakura provides a picturesque backdrop.

Yoritomo claimed descent. As part of the mid-September festival at this shrine, there is a spectacular tournament of archery on horseback *(yabusame)*, in which contestants dressed in the costume of Kamakura period huntsmen must hit a series of three small wooden targets as they come down a narrow course at full gallop. The spacing between the targets gives the rider just barely enough time to drop the reins, notch and fire an arrow, and regain control of his mount.

On the grounds of the shrine are two museums. The **Kamakura Municipal Museum of Modern Art** houses a collection of Japanese oil paintings, watercolors, wood block prints, and sculpture.The **Kokuhokan** (National Treasure Museum) has a fine collection of objects from various Kamakura temples and shrines, including some excellent 13th-century paintings.

The Daibutsu (Great Buddha) in the courtyard of Kotoku-in temple—one of Japan's most important landmarks.

A short walk east from Hachimangu is the **tomb of Yoritomo**—an exceedingly plain and modest affair compared with the way a later dynasty of shoguns chose to immortalize themselves at Nikko. In many ways Yoritomo was a less-than-admirable figure in Japanese history, but you still might want to stop at this little moss-covered stone pagoda to pay your respects.

If for nothing else, Yoritomo earns our admiration for his determination to create a "Seated Buddha" for his capital to rival the huge bronze figure made in 749 for Todaiji temple in Nara. That idea bore fruit in 1292 with the casting of the 120-ton **Daibutsu** in the courtyard of Kotoku in temple   after Mr. Fuji, probably the most photographed icon of Japan. The massive seated figure, 11.4 m (37 ft) high, sits in the classical pose of the Amida Buddha ("Compassionate One"), his hands resting in his lap, the thumbs touching the palms and the eyes half-closed in an expression of profound serenity. The statue is hollow, and you can climb a staircase inside to look out through a window between the Buddha's shoulders. A temple was originally built to house the figure, but this structure was destroyed in a tidal wave in 1495. For the five centuries since then, the Buddha has been dispensing his benevolence to visitors in the open air.

The Daibutsu and Kotoku-in temple are in Hase, the district in the western part of Kamakura. The other major attraction here is **Hasedera**. In the Kannon Hall of this temple is the largest wooden devotional figure in the country: a statue of the "Eleven-Faced Goddess of Mercy," some 10 m (33 ft) high, carved from a single tree trunk and covered in gold leaf. The 10 smaller heads in her crown symbolize her ability to search in all directions for those in need of compassion. No one knows for certain when the figure was carved; one legend dates it to the early 8th century. The Amida Hall of Hasedera houses the image of a seated Amida Buddha, endowed by Minamoto no Yoritomo when he was 42—a particularly unlucky age according to popular Japanese belief. Yoritomo's piety bought him a little more time to enjoy his success; he was 52 when he was thrown by a horse and died of his injuries.

Ryukoji Temple and Enoshima Island

Kamakura history was not shaped by the Minamoto clan alone. No account of this area would be complete without the story of Nichiren (1222–1282), the monk who founded the only native Japanese sect of Buddhism. Nichiren's defiance of both Zen and Jodo ("Pure Land") Buddhism eventually persuaded the shogunate to order him beheaded on a hill to the south of Hase. However, legend says that, just as the executioner raised his sword, a lightning bolt struck and broke it in two. Before he could try again, a messenger arrived with an order commuting Nichiren's sentence to exile on the island of Sadogashima. Later, in 1337, the Nichiren sect built the **Ryukoji** temple on the same hill.

On the nearby Sagami bayshore are Yuigahama and Shichiriga-hama, two of the beaches closest to the metropolitan area. In the hot, humid summer months it can feel as if the entire population of Tokyo and Yokohama is here, searching in vain for a vacant patch of sand. Equally popular is **Enoshima**, the little island just offshore, with a

Shizuka's Dance

The Hachimangu shrine was the scene of many dramatic incidents, including the assassination of Sanetomo, Yorito-mo's second son and the last Minamoto shogun, by his own nephew—a priest named Kugyo. A ginkgo tree by the shrine's main hall marks the spot where the murder took place.

The most poignant tale, however, is associated with the so-called Maiden Hall. Once installed as shogun, Yoritomo fell out with his dashing half-brother Yoshitsune, whom he believed was plotting against him, and sent him into exile. Yoshitsune's lover, Shizuka, was brought to Hachimangu and commanded to dance at the shrine as penance. What she performed, however, was a dance of defiance and love for Yoshitsune. When Yoritomo discovered that Shizuka was carrying Yoshitsune's child, he ordered it killed at birth. But the outcome of this story is lost in legend. Some versions as-sert that the child was indeed slain; others say it was placed in a cradle, like Moses, and cast adrift in the reeds.

hill in the middle that affords—
on clear days—a fine view of
Mt. Fuji and the Izu Peninsula.

Hakone

Hakone is a national park and
resort area southeast of Mt. Fuji,
extremely popular with weekend trippers from Tokyo. Just 90
minutes by train from the city,
this area makes a very pleasant
daytrip. But to enjoy more of the
countryside, you can stay
overnight and continue down
the Izu Peninsula the next day.

Even if you have a Japan
Railpass, we suggest that you
invest in the all-inclusive
"Hakone Free Pass" offered by
the Odakyu Railway. This enti-
tles you to a roundtrip train
ticket from Shinjuku to Gora,
connecting with the funicular
railway up into the mountains
to a cable car. You then swing
across the volcanic Owakudani
valley and down the other side

*Sulfur steam seeps up from the
ground at the Natural Science
Center in Hakone.*

for a boat cruise across Lake Ashi to Hakone-machi. From there,
you can take a bus (still on the same pass) along the Sumiko River to
Odawara, and then back by train to Tokyo.

Among the many attractions of this excursion is the **Hakone**
Open Air Museum (Chokoku no mori, or "Forest of Sculptures") at
Miyanoshita. Established in 1969, the museum rejoices in a wonder-

fully designed and landscaped mountain setting. Here the works of such Western sculptors as Moore, Arp, Calder, and Giacometti share the garden space with those of Shimizu Takashi, Takamura Kotaro, and other Japanese artists. The exhibits are chosen for their resistance to the elements, and the museum is as lovely in winter as it is in summer.

Visitors stop here on the way to the little town of Gora, to catch the cable car to Sozan and from there the gondola ride up into the mountains and across the smoking, sulfurous Owakudani valley. There's a stop en route where you can visit the **Owakudani Natural Science Museum**, which has some uninspiring audio-visual presentations of volcanic eruptions. Down in the basement is the really interesting display: an array of seismographs busily recording the movement of the vast tectonic plates deep below.

Ride the next cable car to the shore of **Lake Ashi**, where excursion cruisers leave from the piers at Togendai for the 20-minute ride to Hakone-machi on the other side of the lake. On a good day the reflection of Mt. Fuji in these clear blue waters is breathtaking. In early August the resorts on the lakeshore sponsor the dramatic Torii Matsuri festival, when a great wooden arch is set alight and a thousand burning lanterns are sent floating out across the water.

Up, up, and away. Take the easy way—cable car—across the volcanic Owakudani valley; then take a boat ride across Lake Ashi.

In the Tokugawa period Hakone-machi was an important town on the Tokaido, the only highway through this mountainous area between the imperial court in Kyoto and the shogunal capital in Edo. The shogunate, always suspicious of people on the move, maintained a system of garrisons along the road, and no one went through without an official pass. The checkpoint here, called the **Hakone**

Sekisho, is an exact replica of the original, with a small museum of period costumes and weapons. The surrounding area is well known for its inns and thermal baths and for its Hakone-zaiku woodcrafts with inlaid mosaic and marquetry.

Izu Peninsula

The jumping-off point for this popular vacation area is the town of Atami, about an hour from Tokyo on the *shinkansen* super-express train. The **Izu Peninsula** is blessed with a sunny climate, fine beaches, picturesque little fishing ports, and—perhaps more to the point —some of the country's best hot springs resorts.

Two of the resort towns are of special interest to Westerners. **Ito**, about 16 km (10 miles) south of Atami on the east coast, is a spa with some 800 thermal springs and good surf swimming along its beautiful, rugged coast. The nearby Omura-san Park has 3,000 cherry trees, with different varieties blooming at different times of year. Historically, Ito was home for five years to William Adams, the Englishman shipwrecked on the shores of Kyushu in the early 17th century who became an advisor to Tokugawa Ieyasu. For his knowledge of seafaring, he was given the title *anjin* ("pilot"). At Ieyasu's command, Adams (the model for the hero of James Clavell's novel *Shogun)* set up a shipyard in Ito and built Japan's first two European-style ocean-going vessels. There is a monument to Adams at the mouth of the Okawa River, and the Anjin Festival is held in his honor every August.

Shimoda, at the southern tip of the peninsula, is famous in still another historical context. It was off the coast here that Commodore Matthew Perry, ordered by the US government to open diplomatic relation with Japan by force if necessary, anchored his fleet of black ships. The shogunate bowed to the pressure and agreed to accept American diplomat Townsend Harris, who established the first US consulate at Gyokusenji temple in Shimoda in 1856. Two years later, at nearby Ryosenji temple, negotiations resulted in the first US–Japan Treaty of Amity and Commerce. The monument to Perry and Harris, not far from the harbor, celebrates these epochal events, as does Shimoda's annual Kurobune Matsuri ("Black Ship Festival") in May.

In fact, charming though it still is today as a fishing port and yacht harbor, Shimoda was worthless from the commercial or diplomatic perspective. The shogunate had simply stuck Harris there to keep the dreaded Westerners away from the capital. Later, he negotiated the opening of Yokohama as a trading port and foreign settlement. Such was the subsequent dismay among reactionary factions at this sign of weakness that the Tokugawa shogunate was soon overthrown.

Mt. Fuji

Most of the world's national symbols—the Statue of Liberty, the Eiffel Tower, the Kremlin, the Great Wall—are man-made. Japan's is a phenomenon of nature. And yet, in its near perfect symmetry, the cone of **Mt. Fuji**, snowcapped even in summer, is so exquisitely formed that it seems more like the work of an infinitely patient landscape artist than a volcanic accident. The solitary majestic peak rises 3,776 m (12,385 ft) into the heavens. It is, in a word, simply beautiful. Here, more than in any temple garden or ancient castle ground, you can appreciate why the Japanese prefer to blur the distinction between nature and art.

The volcano's name is thought to derive from an Ainu word for "fire." Fuji-san last erupted in 1707, and today only an occasional puff of steam breaks through its crust, the fitful snore of a sleeping giant. Graciously, it remains dormant for the sake of the hundreds of thousands of visitors who come every year to climb to the summit.

For some, the climb is an act of piety: the mountain is revered as the abode of Japan's ancestral gods. For others, the climb is an exercise in self-discipline and physical purification. Still others come out of no particular religious impulse, on holiday, making the ascent mainly to be able to say they've done it and leaving—almost in spite of themselves—with a profound sense of spiritual uplift. No travel

brochure can make Mt. Fuji a cliché, nor can the most jaded of world travelers remain immune.

Most visitors begin their climb at Kawaguchi Lake, in the resort area north of the mountain, getting that far by train from Tokyo in about two hours. The official climbing season is 1 July to 31 August, although mountain huts at each of the ten stations on the various routes of ascent are open from April to mid-November. Climbing "out of season" (especially in wet weather) is not recommended, but people do it all the time.

From Kawaguchi, you take a local bus to Go-gome ("Fifth Station") on the north face, to start the five-hour hike to the summit. There's also a direct bus to this point from the Shinjuku bus terminal in Tokyo that takes about two and a half hours. If you're coming from Kyoto or Osaka, the train or bus connections bring you to the Fujino-miya trail, on the south face.

Truly dedicated pilgrims begin the climb around midnight, reaching the top in time to greet the sunrise. There's no danger of losing the well-marked trail, and the **night** ascent obviates the need to put up at any of the dormitory-style mountain huts along the way (where the accommodations are truly awful). You can stop at the seventh or eighth station to rest en route. Pack extra-warm clothing and wear good hiking boots, hats, and gloves. Bad junk food from vending machines is all that's available at the summit, so it's best to bring your own supplies and, above all, a thermos of hot tea or coffee.

Fuji-san is like any other mountain in one respect: it's a lot easier coming down. More adventurous visitors will take the descent down the volcanic sand slide called the *suna-bashiri* to Shin-Go-gome ("New Fifth Station"). Just sit on your backpack or a piece of cardboard, push off, and slither down. From Shin-Go-gome, buses connect to the town of Gotemba for connections home.

Morning glow: rowing on a still lake under the peak
of Mt. Fuji.

Don't confine your visit to the mountain only. The **Fuji Five Lakes** that form a crescent around the north side of the peak offer delightful opportunities for fishing, boating, and hiking. Yamanaka-ko is the largest of the five. Kawaguchi-ko is the most popular, probably because of the excursion boats that ply the route along the north shore, where—with luck and good weather—you get a perfect mirror-image reflection of Mt. Fuji in the water. Sai-ko has the best trout fishing, and Shoji-ko is smallest, prettiest, and still relatively undeveloped. Motosu-ko is the clearest and deepest of the five.

Between Sai-ko and Shoji-ko lies the dense, mysterious **Jukai** ("Sea of Trees"), a forest notorious for being easier to enter than to leave. The volcanic substrata here throw magnetic compasses completely out of whack. Many holiday visitors lose their way, some of them on purpose: the eerie Jukai is a perennial favorite with would-be suicides, and every year the local authorities conduct a sweep of the forest to recover the bodies that would otherwise never be discovered. Due south of Motosu-ko, the glistening white 26-m (85-ft) Shiraito Falls make a far more cheerful setting for a picnic.

KANSAI

Embracing the historical and cultural centers of Kyoto and Nara, the Ise-Shima shrines, and the vibrant commercial cities of Osaka and Kobe, the **Kansai** region is essentially the heart of the nation.

While Tokyo usually provides the first glimpse of modern Japan's many strange contrasts, it is to Kyoto and Nara that visitors with even a passing interest in Japanese history and culture come to peel back the layers of centuries. Although Kyoto is internationally renowned as the country's de facto cultural capital, nearby Nara was the first important home of the imperial court and still boasts many of Japan's most important temples and shrines.

Ise-Shima National Park is the supreme sanctuary of Japan's ancestral Shinto deities. Osaka and neighboring Kobe offer striking perspectives of modern commercial Japan, albeit on a more accessible and less intimidating scale than Tokyo's sprawling urban conglomeration. No other region of Japan offers the same combination of urban intensity, rural tranquillity, and dramatic cultural treasures —and all in such close proximity.

Kyoto

For millions of would-be travelers around the world, the very name **Kyoto** conjures up images of the exotic and the foreign. Here you will find magnificent temples, shrines, and pagodas; exquisite Zen gardens; sumptuous traditional feasts; and, of course, that most alluring and misunderstood of creatures—the kimono-clad geisha. Kyoto is the national center for such traditional disciplines as *cha-do* (tea

---

Kyoto Museums

Kyoto Museum of Traditional Crafts

9-1 Seishoji-cho, Okazaki, Sakyo-ku; Tel. (075) 762-2670. Open 10am–6pm daily except Mondays. Free admission.

Costume Museum 5th fl., Izutus Bldg., Shin-Hanayacho-Horikawa-kado, Shimogyo-ku; Tel. (075) 361-8388. Open 9am–5pm daily except Sundays. Admission ¥400.

Kyoto National Museum 527 Chayamachi, Higashiyama-ku; Tel. (075) 541-1151. Open daily December–March 9am–4:30pm, April–November 9am–8pm; closed Mondays. Admission ¥420 (adults), ¥130 (students), ¥70 (children).

Miho Museum take train from Kyoto Station to JR Ishiyama Station, then 50 minutes on the Teisan bus line. Open 10am–5pm daily except Mondays, 10am–8pm on Saturdays (open in spring from 15 March to 10 June, in summer 21 July to 16 August, and in autumn 1 September to 15 December). Admission ¥1,000 (adults), ¥800 (students), ¥300 (children).

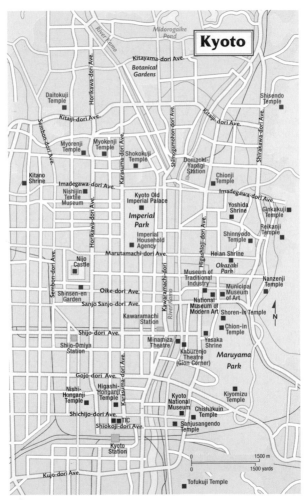

Kyoto

River Kamo

Midorogaike Pond

Kitayama-dori Ave.

Botanical Gardens

Horikawa-dori Ave.

Daitokuji Temple

Shisendo Temple

Kitaiji-dori Ave.

Kitaiji-dori Ave.

Sembon-dori Ave.

Myorenji Temple

Myokenji Temple

Shimogamohon-dori Ave.

Karasuma-dori Ave.

Shokokuji Temple

Shirakawa-dori Ave.

Kitano Shrine

Imadegawa-dori Ave.

Demachi-Yanagi Station

Chionji Temple

Imadegawa-dori Ave.

Nishijin Textile Museum

Kyoto Old Imperial Palace

Yoshida Shrine

Ginkakuji Temple

Horikawa-dori Ave.

Imperial Park

Reikanji Temple

Imperial Household Agency

Shinnyodo Temple

Heian Shrine

Sembon-dori Ave.

Nijo Castle

Marutamachi-dori Ave.

Higashioji-dori Ave.

Nanzenji Temple

Shinsen-en Garden

Oike-dori Ave.

Museum of Traditional Industry

Okazaki Park

Municipal Museum of Art

Sanjo Sanjo-dori Ave.

Kawaramachi-dori

River Kamo

National Museum of Modern Art

Shoren-in Temple

N

Kawaramachi Station

Chion-in Temple

Shijo-dori Ave.

Yasaka Shrine

Shijo-Omiya Station

Minamiza Theatre

Maruyama Park

Kaburenjo Theatre (Gion Corner)

Gojo-dori Ave.

Karasuma-dori Ave.

Nishi-Honganji Temple

Higashi-Honganji Temple

Kyoto National Museum

Kiyomizu Temple

Shichijo-dori Ave.

Chishakuin Temple

TIC

Shiokoji-dori Ave.

Sanjusangendo Temple

Kyoto Station

0   1500 m

0   1500 yards

Kujo-dori Ave.

Tofukuji Temple

92

ceremony) and *ikebana* (flower arranging), the birthplace of *kabuki,* and the leading center of calligraphy, painting, and sculpture.

The city has a unique place in the Japanese national identity, and one-third of Japan's entire population is estimated to visit the city each year. Despite this, in many ways Kyoto is a surprisingly typical modern Japanese city, with the usual nondescript concrete buildings along with the remarkable pockets of culture and beauty.

For a thousand years, Kyoto served as the cultural and spiritual capital of Japanese civilization, the home of its revered emperors after the Nara period from the end of the 8th century up to the Meiji Restoration in the late-19th century. The imperial rulers moved the capital to Kyoto originally to escape from the growing domination of the Buddhist authorities of Nara. In the new capital the building of Buddhist temples was actually briefly banned—ironic in a city now universally renowned for its temples.

Kyoto simply means "Capital City," though it was originally known as Heian-kyo ("Capital of Peace"), the name given to the golden Heian era between the tenth and 12th centuries. During this time Kyoto thrived as Japan's cultural and creative heartland. But the city's fortunes turned during the Warring States period (1467–1568), which was finally ended by the unifying warlords Nobunaga and Hideyoshi in the mid-16th century.

In many ways the city has never recovered from Hideyoshi's subsequent decision to move the national capital from Kyoto to Edo (now Tokyo) in the early 1600s—a blow compounded by the young Emperor Meiji shifting the imperial household to Tokyo in 1868. But Kyoto has nevertheless remained the repository of the nation's noblest cultural pursuits and architectural legacy.

Kyoto's Imperial Residences

The Imperial Palace (Kyoto Gosho) and the Katsura and Shugakuin imperial villas are mandatory destinations for anyone with even a shred of interest in Japanese architecture, design, and aesthetics. How-

ever, since they are imperial property, special reservations must be made with the Kyoto office of the Imperial Household Agency (located on the grounds of the Imperial Palace, just south of Imadegawa-dori; passports are required). Overseas reservations are not accepted.

Fires ravaged Kyoto's original 8th century **Imperial Palace**, and the present buildings are a 19th-century reconstruction. Through the western Seishomon Gate is the Shishinden ceremonial hall, where emperors are enthroned—a privilege retained by Kyoto after the move to Tokyo—and where New Year's audiences are held. To the west is the cypress-wood Seiryoden (the "Serene and Cool Chamber"), the emperor's private chapel, serene and cool indeed in vermilion, white, and black.

If you must visit only one of the two imperial villas, **Katsura** is the ultimate "must see" in a city full of them. Conceived with meticulous care, Katsura is one of Japan's masterpieces of subtle residential design and garden landscaping. Every wall in the villa's seven pavilions is a sliding panel that can be opened to survey the surrounding landscape, including the gardens themselves and the Arashiyama Hills beyond. The Furushoin pavilion's verandah is the perfect place for viewing the full moon.

The **Shugakuin** imperial villa lies at the foot of sacred Mt. Hici. Its spacious grounds are a magnificent example of the "strolling" gardens favored during the Edo period. Built by the shogun in the 17th century for an abdicated emperor, Shugakuin is in fact three villas, each with airy teahouses in the gardens. The upper villa—grandest of the three—dominates an imposing avenue of pines.

Exploring the City

Kyoto is surprisingly large. Since its numerous attractions are spread evenly throughout the city, good maps are essential. The city has two

Giant torii arch near the Heian Shrine in Kyoto—the city is home to some 200 Shinto shrines and over 1,500 Buddhist temples.

subway lines, several small private railway lines, and many bus routes. If you don't want to depend on costly taxis, make sure you have a bus map, which can be picked up at the tourist information offices in Kyoto Station or at any JNTO office. However, with over 1,500 Buddhist temples, 200 Shinto shrines, numerous museums, and magnificent imperial palaces, be aware that you're not going to see everything.

Try to get hold of the *Kyoto Visitor's Guide,* a free glossy monthly packed with listings of cultural events and information on temples, gardens, festivals, exhibitions, restaurants, and even accommodation.

Sampling Kyoto is definitely a case of "less is more." The secret is to pace yourself. It is far better to allow a daily ration of a couple of major temples, a museum, and a strolling garden or two than to cram everything into a short time, leaving only a blur of each and a lasting impression of none.

Higashiyama

On the city's east side, **Higashiyama** boasts temples, theaters, museums, and parks—a fine introduction to exploring the imperial city on foot.

Kiyomizu temple, one of Kyoto's oldest, is so popular that on Sundays it offers all the serenity of rush hour at Kyoto's garish new station. But don't let that put you off. Founded in 788 just before the city entered its golden age as the imperial capital, its numerous buildings nestle lovingly against steep Mt. Higashiyama in a dramatic cascade of thatched and tiled roofs. However, most of what we see today is actually a 17th-century reconstruction of the original 8th-century structure. With its numerous buildings set within extensive grounds, Kiyomizu's main attraction is the *hondo* (main hall). This elevated structure's projecting wooden terrace is supported by a vast arrangement of 139 massive interlocking beams. Across on the mountainside is another terrace on which imperial courtiers and dignitaries would sit while enjoying dance performances and music recitals on the *hondo's* broad terrace. (The popular expression "To

Apprentice geisha making tea in Kyoto, a city suffused with Japanese traditions and customs.

jump from Kiyomizu's terrace" means to do something daring and adventurous, although this is best left to the imagination.)

Crowds flock here to take in the bright yet delicate hues of cherry blossoms in spring or the blaze of red and gold maple leaves in autumn, with special night-time illuminations (check at any tourist office for dates and times).

A moderate stroll takes you to Higashiyama's **Gion** district, Kyoto's main historical center of traditional theater, arts, and (now) antiques. It is especially renowned as the last center of training for the city's most celebrated residents, the geisha. This is the place to wander and soak up the sights and sounds of Kyoto's lone quarter still dedicated to traditional arts and entertainment. Your curiosity

Those Enigmatic Geisha

Few aspects of Japanese life are more elusive than the geisha. You might see cheap imitations in expensive night-clubs on Tokyo's Ginza or even a real one being driven past in a limousine on the way to an exclusive party. But as a non-Japanese, you are unlikely to see an authentic geisha first-hand unless you find yourself the guest of a Japanese businessman with a very fat expense account. It is usually unheard of for them to perform for unescorted foreigners, who are not considered sufficiently versed in Japanese ways to appreciate the finer points of this time-honored institution.

The word geisha means "talented person" — in Kyoto, as befits the old imperial capital, she's more elegantly known as *geiko* ("talented lady"). She has the sophisticated talents of a singer, dancer, actress, and musician. A girl is taken on in her teens as an apprentice and is carefully trained by older geisha in the traditional arts of entertaining Japanese men who want to spend an evening in an elegant tea-house, away from their wives.

Contrary to popular conception, a geisha is not a glori-fied prostitute. A genuine geisha has the prestige and admi-ration accorded to actresses or singers at the top of their profession in the West. Charm and personality are consid-ered more important than physical beauty. A true geisha is primarily a highly trained professional entertainer, hired on the basis of her charm and skills. Casual affairs with gen-uine customers almost never happen, as these would sully the geisha's all-important reputation.

and patience will inevitably reward you with a glimpse of a genuine geisha or *maiko* (apprentice geisha), the copious layers of her opulent—and unimaginably heavy—silk kimono rustling as she hurries to an appointment or a training session.

Gion is a global magnet for collectors and dealers of Japanese antiques. Prices are usually high. But even if you're not in the market for a major investment, antique-store browsing is a marvelous way to get a real taste of Japan's celebrated traditional design and aesthetics. Some stores are more like small museums, offering exquisite examples of the finest craftsmanship.

The 17th-century Minamiza Theater—Japan's oldest—stages the famous Kaomise *kabuki* show in December. But foreign visitors can enjoy the **Gion Corner**, held at Yasaka Hall to provide a selection of bite-sized samples of Japanese culture from March through November. In a comfortable little theater you can watch a one-hour demonstration of tea ceremony, traditional music and dance, flower arranging, puppet theater, and a *kyogen* farce. (Tickets for Gion Corner are usually available through your hotel or the Tourist Information Center.)

At the northeast corner of Gion is **Maruyama Park**, one of Kyoto's most popular recreation areas, which borders two important temples. The massive **Chioninji** is home to the Jodo ("Pure Land") Buddhist sect, which in the 12th century spread the appeal of Buddhism to the uneducated classes. Looming to an imposing height of 24 m (79 ft), its entrance gate is thought to be the largest structure of its kind in the world. The ringing of Chioninji's bell, Japan's largest and best known, is televised nationally when resident monks usher in the new year.

A huge arch *(torii)* spanning the main road marks the approach to the **Heian Shrine**. This popular shrine features a strongly Chinese-influenced design and an extensive landscaped garden considered one of Kyoto's finest, with numerous cherry trees and a large pond with an elegant pagoda linked to the shore by a covered bridge.

In the vicinity are two absorbing museums reflecting Kyoto's extensive history as a magnet for Japan's finest craftsmen. The **Museum of Traditional Industry** presents a diverse collection of textiles, porcelain, fans, dolls, lacquerware, cutlery, and cabinetwork, with occasional live demonstrations by craftsmen. Next door, the **National Museum of Modern Art** is, despite its name, mainly devoted to 19th- and 20th-century ceramics.

At the northern edge of Higashiyama is one of Japan's most famous and delightful short walks: the **Philosopher's Path**, stretching along a canal running between two major temples—Nanzenji and Ginkakuji.

Nanzenji is a former 13th-century palace whose precincts now house a dozen affiliated temples and monasteries. The great gate at the main entrance was built in 1628 and became notorious as the site where a robber named Goemon Ishikawa was boiled alive in an iron cauldron while holding his son aloft to save him from the same fate. Since then, old-fashioned Japanese iron bathtubs have been gruesomely known as "goemon-buro." The view from atop the 30-m (98-ft) gate provides a fine overall view of the temple grounds and sacred Mt. Hiei to the north. The temple's truly

Philosopher's Path stretches between the Ginkakuji and Nanzenji temples.

All the World's a Garden

In a Japanese garden, every artifice is used to make things look "natural." By cunning use of proportion, designers are able to make a small space appear to be a vast landscape. Gardens might be formal, semiformal, or informal—the same concepts that characterize Japanese painting and flower arrangement.

Influenced by the Chinese, the Japanese have been designing their ingenious garden landscapes since the sixth century. Later, under the influence of the austere precepts of Zen Buddhism, gardens encouraged meditation, as in the peaceful rock-and-water garden of Kamakura's Zuisenji temple.

The Zen garden reached its zenith in Kyoto with "flat gardens" devoid of hills, bridges, or ponds—only rocks in white sand or gravel. The most famous is at Ryoanji temple, but equally admirable examples can be seen at Nanzenji's "Leaping Tiger Garden" or Zuiho-in's "Blissful Mountain."

More elaborate designs evolved to incorporate existing natural features. The opulent Momoyama architecture at the end of the 16th century brought dramatic and colorful gardens with bizarrely shaped rocks and trees, as at Kyoto's Nishi-Honganji temple.

Edo garden design became more utilitarian—with fruit trees to provide food and reeds for making arrows. Larger, so-called strolling gardens came close to the spirit of English parks, but still with deliberate aesthetic touches, as in the celebrated Kenrokuen garden in Kanazawa or the Ritsurin Park in Takamatsu on Shikoku island.

Japanese gardens have something even for our industrial age. Offices sometimes boast tray-gardens with miniature bonsai trees, pebble-rocks, and even a tiny goldfish pond. Technicians are even working on gardens for the first Japanese spacecraft.

unique feature is the large red-brick aqueduct behind the main buildings, which still carries water from Lake Biwa and is a popular strolling route for local residents.

Not far from Nanzenji is the wonderful **Eikan-do**, an exquisite temple set against the hillside. Its beautiful Amida Buddha statue is, unusually, turning to look back over its shoulder. Its strange posture commemorates a legendary statue that came to life and then berated Eikan, the astonished monk looking on, for pausing from his ritual chanting. Each fall the temple has a special night-time illumination of its many maple trees, their flaming reds and oranges highlighted with strategically placed pin-spotlights. The effect is sublime and utterly unforgettable.

Despite the large numbers who come to view the spring blossoms and the superb fall leaves, the Philosopher's Path is one of Kyoto's most tranquil and beloved strolls. Any of the several friendly little teahouses and coffee shops along the way make an ideal rest stop.

A teahouse is usually designed by the tea master himself and situated in a secluded area partitioned off from the rest of the garden.

At the other end of the canal is the second major temple on the path. **Ginkakuji**, the famous "Silver Pavilion," never received the silver-leaf covering originally intended. It was built in the 15th century by an aesthete-mystic shogun, Yoshimasa Ashikaga, who used it for esoteric tea ceremonies and, above all, moon-watching in the elegant garden. Its flat-topped hillock of white gravel, despite the inevitable comparison to Mt. Fuji, reputedly originated as a pile of sand left behind by the temple's construction workers.

A short bus ride delivers you to the **Kyoto National Museum**, which houses the country's largest collection of Japanese sculpture and painting as well as weapons, traditional armor, and ten centuries of costume including some dazzling noh theater costumes with masks. Most of this peerless collection has been gathered from the temples and palaces of Kyoto, Nara, and other important cultural centers.

The Fushimi Inari shrines, with rice and fox motifs throughout, are among the most dazzling shrines in southern Kyoto.

Just south of the National Museum is the spectacular **Sanjusan-gendo**, the "Hall of Thirty-Three Bays." The original temple built in 1164 survived only 100 years, and today's reconstruction dates from the 13th century. Its centerpiece is a gilded seated wooden statue of the Kannon Bodhisattva, 3.3 m (11 ft) high, with 11 faces on the crown of its head and 40 arms (extravagantly known as "a thousand arms") wielding bells, wheels, and lotus flowers. However, Sanju-sangendo's main wonder is its legion of 1,000 gilded Kannon images flanking the central Buddha. The identical statues were carved by the 13th-century masters Kokei, Unkei, and Tankei, ably aided by 70 assistants.

Ukyo and Kita

These districts on the west and north sides of Kyoto are home to most of the city's major temples, set within the surrounding greenery and mountains that prompted the Emperor Kammu to select this site for his new capital, Heian-kyo, in 794.

Nestled in the northwest corner of Kyoto, **Ryoanji** is the best known of all Zen Buddhist temples. Its famous rock garden has provoked more debates—both admiring and critical—than there are

chips of gravel in its rectangular 30-m by 10-m (98-ft by 32-ft) expanse. There are no trees and no shrubs, just 15 stark rocks embellished with ancient moss, standing in clusters amid the perfectly raked white gravel. Although it is usually attributed to the great master Soami, nobody knows for sure who created it—or why. The mystery surrounding its origins does nothing to undermine the power of its simplicity. Confounding interpretation, it epitomizes the essence of Zen Buddhism's essentially anti-intellectual precepts. Dark islands in a white sea, or mountain peaks soaring above

clouds: people see what they want to see. Get there early in the morning before the crowds arrive. Kyoto offers few more memorable experiences than secluded contemplation of Ryoanji's enigmatic rock garden.

Beyond the rock garden you can walk among the maples and pines of the forest surrounding the lovely Kyoyochi Pond at the foot of Mt. Kinugasa. Thick, luxuriant moss thrives throughout.

From Ryoanji, a 20-minute stroll or a short bus ride takes you to **Kinkakuji**, Japan's famous "Temple of the Golden Pavilion." The original late-14th-century pavilion, completely covered in gold leaf, was

Meditate on this—the Zen rock garden of Tofukuji is yet another pocket of tranquility.

typical of the unrestrained opulence of the Muromachi period favored by Shogun Yoshimitsu Ashikaga, who had it built for his retirement at the ripe old age of 38. It was burned down by a fanatical young monk in 1950, rebuilt in 1955 as an exact replica of the original structure, and renovated in 1987 with a brand new gold-foil covering. Most of its buildings are closed to the public, but you pass an attractive thatch-roofed tea-ceremony house as you follow the winding stone steps toward the exit.

Another celebrated victim of fire is **Daitokuji**. This vast complex of 22 subtemples and affiliated monasteries (down from about 60 during the Edo period) was built, burned down, and rebuilt between the 14th and 17th centuries. It is richly endowed with artistic treasures and some of Japan's most superb Zen gardens, reflecting its history as a renowned center of calligraphy, gardening, tea ceremony, and other refined arts.

Four of Daitokuji's Zen subtemples in particular offer superb gardens, teahouses, and artifacts. Daisen-in, the "Zen Temple Without Equal," contains splendid painted *fusuma* (sliding panels) and wall paintings. Zuiho-in is a monastery whose curious gardens combine Zen Buddhist and Christian symbolism, together with both an attractive rock garden and a unusually geometric tea garden. Ryugen-in has five distinct rock gardens, one of which is apparently the smallest in Japan.

West of Daisen-in is the **Juko-in** monastery, where Sen no Rikyu, the founder of the tea ceremony and its most celebrated master, is buried. His death in 1591 by *seppuku* (the ritual disemboweling more crudely known to Westerners as *harakiri)* was in fact commanded by Toyotomi Hideyoshi, his former friend and patron. Rikyu apparently incurred the warlord's wrath by placing a statue of himself in the large main gate, under which Hideyoshi would have had to pass—an intolerable affront to a famously proud warrior.

To the south is **Kitano Temmangu**, a large and important shrine. Temmangu shrines around the country typically feature statues of seated cows and bulls believed to have healing properties. You will always see someone rubbing the part of a statue corresponding to an afflicted area in the hope of relief from pain and worry. The shrine is also known for its thousands of plum trees, whose deep pink blooms draw the crowds in the weeks preceding the annual cherry blossom frenzy. But the real crowds descend on the 25th of each month, when Kitano Temmangu hosts its nationally famous flea market. People travel from afar to sift through the offerings of used kimono, antique furniture and ceramics, antique scrolls, crafts, food, household items, and countless other categories of bric-a-brac and sundries, paying prices ranging from the reasonable to the outrageous.

Central Kyoto

To the southwest of Kyoto Station is **Toji**, one of Kyoto's oldest temples, whose massive pagoda is the largest in Japan. Toji was established just after the imperial capital moved to Kyoto in 794, built with wood from sacred Mt. Inari in the south. Thirty years later Kukai, the revered founder of esoteric Shingon Buddhism, was appointed head abbot. The temple complex quickly became Kyoto's main center of Shingon Buddhism, which it remains today. In addition to its impressive pagoda, Toji is a national magnet for bargain hunters at its huge monthly flea market held on the 21st of each month.

Just north of the tower are the headquarters of two schools of the Jodo-Shinshu ("Pure Land") sect, the Nishi-Honganji and Higashi-Honganji temples. The latter was built by Shogun Ieyasu Tokugawa to split and counteract the powerful influence of Nishi-Honganji, which had attracted thousands of followers with its free-wheeling Buddhism: it allowed priests to marry and have children, permitted the eating of meat, and renounced traditional ascetic practices.

Most of **Higashi-Honganji** is closed to the public, but the main hall and founder's hall, rebuilt in 1895 after repeated fires, are notable for the rather gross ropes of human hair fashioned from donations by female worshippers to haul the temple's pillars into position. There is much more to see in nearby **Nishi-Honganji**, an

outstanding example of Japanese Buddhist monumental architecture, combining a bold, dramatic silhouette with rich ornamentation. The 17th-century buildings owe much of their splendor to the structures brought here from Hideyoshi's opulent Fushimi Castle on the south side of Kyoto (dismantled by a Tokugawa shogun in 1632).

Nijo Castle is a poignant monument to the ironic twists of history. Built by Ieyasu Tokugawa in 1603 for his occasional, reluctant visits to Kyoto (under imperial command), the castle was taken over by the Emperor Meiji after the restoration of 1868. It was here that the emperor signed the edict abolishing the shogunate and sent his

Moat, outer wall, and gateway of Nijo Castle—reminders of days before visiting hours existed.

carpenters round the castle to replace the Tokugawa hollyhock crest with the imperial chrysanthemum.

For a change of pace and mood, seek out **Nishiki Market**. This remarkably tranquil street market is housed under a single arcade. Note the colorful stands of dried fish and fresh fish, colorful pickles, stout young bamboo shoots, chicken wings and breasts arranged in elaborate patterns, and a whole cornucopia of squid, mussels, oysters, and giant scallops.

Nearby, leading north from Shiji-dori, is another important market area worth exploring: **Teramachi** (literally, "temple district").

Hideyoshi moved many of Kyoto's temples to this long narrow road during his reorganization of the city in 1591 following its near-total destruction by clan warfare. Although small temples and shrines remain, visitors will enjoy exploring the covered shopping arcade between Shijo and Sanjo streets, famous for its second-hand bookstores, traditional hand-made paper *(washi)* shops, trendy but sometimes creative clothing stores, and numerous pickle shops.

North of Oike, Teramachi becomes home to some of Kyoto's most respected antique and *washi* shops, some of which have been in business for hundreds of years. The adjoining streets comprise one of Japan's finest centers for traditional Japanese style tables, screens, lamps, scrolls, and other refined furnishings.

South Kyoto

It is impossible to overstate the importance of rice in Japanese culture. Each year in an important ceremony, the emperor plants rice in a symbolic field, reinforcing his role as the hereditary link between the Japanese people and their Shinto gods. So important is rice that it has the Shinto deity Inari all to itself. There are thousands of Inari shrines throughout Japan, distinguished by a pair of foxes standing guard.

> **Outside his room, Shogun Ieyasu had a floor constructed with boards that squeaked with the warble of a nightingale whenever anybody approached along the corridor.**

 Kyoto, however, boasts the most famous of them all—the **Fushimi-Inari Shrine** in southern Kyoto. In a city overpopulated by must-see attractions, this is one place guaranteed to deplete whatever superlatives remain in your exhausted vocabulary. The main shrine buildings are among Kyoto's most extensive, with rice and fox motifs everywhere. But take the path at the top right of the compound and you come to the first of Fushimi-Inari's remarkable features: its long, meandering tunnels of bright orange torii arches. Purchased by both companies and individuals (at vast expense) in the hope of incurring the blessings of the gods, the torii become smaller as you progress through the tunnel and begin to ascend the mountain. Farther on you come to an amazing double tunnel, forcing you to choose the left or right paths. Along the way to the top of Mt. Inari, you will pass many subshrines and countless bright red torii both minute and massive. Make sure you have plenty of film — you'll need it all.

North of Fushimi is **Tofukuji**, a major Zen temple complex. In addition to many impressive buildings, Tofukuji offers four remarkable and distinctive Zen gardens located in the *hojo* (abbot's quarters). At Tofukuji's center is a ravine containing a small forest of maple trees. Hundreds of thousands come each fall to view the spectacular fall colors from the temple's covered Tsutenkyo ("Heavenly Way Bridge").

Excursions from Kyoto

Arashiyama. When mind and body are ready for a break from the rigors of cultural sightseeing, head down to the southern resort district of **Arashiyama**, perched along the Hozu River (or the Oi, as it's also known). The maple trees setting off the river and the famous old wooden Togetsukyo Bridge make it very popular with local tourists, so it is worth avoiding on Sundays and public holidays.

Arashiyama is home to a number of important shrines and temples. The **Nonomiya Shrine** is uniquely renowned for its special role in preparing imperial princesses to serve as vestal virgins at the Grand Shrine of Ise, Japan's most important Shinto shrine (see page 9). The shrine has a prominent role in the *Tale of Genji* and in a famous noh play (titled simply *Nonomiya),* and thus attracts people with especial interest in classical Japanese literature.

Ohara. Also north of Kyoto is the rural enclave of Ohara, home to the magnificent temple complex of **Sanzen'in**. From the bus station, signs in English point the way to the path winding along a stream, past many stalls and small shops selling Ohara's famous pickles, to the temple's massive front gate.

Ohara's Shuhekein pond garden at Sanzen-in in Kyoto, a legendary spot for year-round meditation and contemplation.

The superbly landscaped Shuhekein pond garden is a legendary spot for meditation and contemplation in every season. After the garden, venture into the hall at the end of the corridor and try your hand with a calligraphy brush along with the Japanese visitors writing traditional prayers to the central Amida Buddha. The view of the lush mossy landscaped garden from the verandah at the back of the building is one of Kyoto's most famous. The Ojo Gokurakuin hall at the temple's center contains a magnificent seated Amida Buddha dating from 986 (and so revered that no photography is permitted). The stamps at the various numbered stations throughout the complex are particularly elegant and make a fine and unusual souvenir of your visit.

Miho Museum. Some 30 km (18.5 miles) outside Kyoto, set deep in a forested nature preserve, is the **Miho Museum**, designed by internationally acclaimed architect I.M. Pei. A tunnel leads to this outstanding privately owned collection of ancient Egyptian, South Asian, Chinese, Persian and, of course, Japanese masterworks. The building's exterior, interior and exhibit displays are triumphs of design and harmony between old and new, East and West, simplicity and complexity. The Miho is not to be missed by anyone interested in Asian art and design, both ancient and modern.

Fukui

Just north of Kyoto is **Fukui**, a prefecture long renowned for its unique combination of history and superb natural scenery. For centuries it has been called the Echizen region, and that culturally significant name has definitely stuck. The Echizen coast includes famous columnar rock formations at Tojimbo and Sotomo, as well as some of Japan's finest beaches. Culinary delights include Echizen crab and distinctive Echizen *soba*. And the simple, natural style of Echizen pottery has been popular throughout the country for hundreds of years, as have Echizen's highly regarded lacquerware and hand-crafted knives.

Historical heritage is very much the theme at **Ichidani**. Preserved here is an entire 16th century village that served as the headquarters of the Asakura clan, which ruled Echizen until 1573. The painstakingly recreated buildings contain exhibits of the trades and crafts of the day, including a dyer's workshop, a merchant's office, and samurai homes.

In Fukui's far north, **Awara Onsen** has become one of Japan's most popular hot-spring resort towns since the emperor made it a hot spot for an imperial soak. But don't expect the rustic quaintness of traditional-style inns. Awara typically packs its heat-seekers into modern, luxury hotels whose harsh concrete exteriors hardly reflect the tranquilizing pleasures provided within.

Nara

Although Kyoto remains the country's major cultural and historic destination, Japanese tourists equally revere the Kansai region's other celebrated historical center. **Nara** was Japan's first imperial capital, and it remains home to many of its most important temples, shrines, and collections of Buddhist art treasures. For anyone interested in Japanese history, art, and culture, no visit to Japan could possibly be complete without a glimpse of Nara, however frustratingly brief. And, in addition to its magnificent cultural treasures, Nara offers the unlikely phenomenon of the world's most aggressive deer.

The Kintetsu Station is the ideal starting point for any exploration of the city. Next to the station's south entrance is an excellent tourist information center. The friendly staff usually speak reasonable English and will happily ply you with maps and brochures, help you get oriented, and provide advice and information on festivals and special events.

Next to the fountain outside Kintetsu Station is bustling Higashi-muki-dori, a covered mall of souvenirs shops, antique stores, and numerous eateries. At the other end is Sanjo-dori, Nara's main shopping street, with more of the same plus calligraphy stores noted for their fine inkstones, a Nara specialty.

Nara Park and Mt. Wakakusa

The historic area of Nara is on the east side of the modern town, at the end of Sanjo-dori. **Naramachi** is a famous quarter filled with gorgeous historic houses, small shops, eclectic galleries, and interesting museums. Here too is the western entrance to **Nara Park**, marking the boundary between urban sprawl and primal forest. The town's temples and shrines and a major museum are all encompassed by the park.

Nara Park's most famous residents are its deer, protected since the eighth century, when they were considered messengers from the gods. Despite being wild, the deer are quite tame and loiter around the park's various tourist attractions, hoping for a free snack of the deer biscuits sold here. Have your camera ready to record the incredible sight of a wailing Japanese child beating a hasty retreat to its parents after being chased by a group of hungry deer in a feeding frenzy.

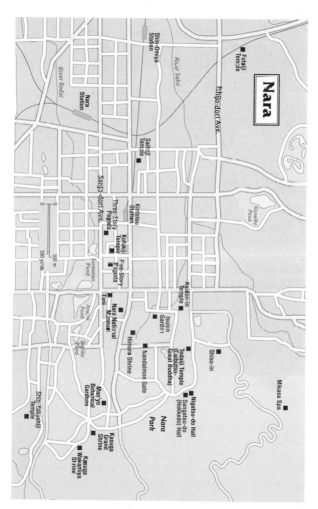

Nara

Shin-Omiya Station

Futaiji Temple

River Saho

Eijo-dori Ave.

River Bodai

Nara Station

Saihoji Temple

Sanjo-dori Ave.

Konishe Pond

Kintetsu Station

Three-Story Pagoda

Kofukuji Temple

Five-Story Pagoda

Saragawa Pond

Kaidan-in Temple

Isuien Garden

Todaiji Temple (Daibutsu-Great Buddha)

Shiso-in

Aruike Pond

Nara National Museum

Himuro Shrine

Seville Pond

Nandaimon Gate

Sangatsu-do (Hokkedo) Hall Nigatsu-do Hall

Mikasa Spa

Shin-Yakushiji Temple

Man'yo Botanical Gardens

Nara Park

Kasuga Grand Shrine

Kasuga Wakamiya Shrine

0   500 yards
0   500 m

Nara Park's most famous residents are its deer, protected since the eighth century—when they were considered messengers of the gods.

At the edge of Sarusawa-ike pond is **Kofukuji** temple. Its imposing 50-m (166-ft) five-story pagoda, Japan's second-largest after Toji in Kyoto, is one of Nara's most photographed images. The present structure dates from 1426, replacing five earlier pagodas destroyed by fire. At its height Kofukuji embraced around 175 separate buildings, including the Kasuga Grand Shrine at the foot of Mt. Wakakusa, with which it has been closely associated for 1,100 years. Kofukuji's many surviving artworks and artifacts are housed in its newest building, the Museum of National Treasures, a fire-proof repository built in 1958 to honor Kofukuji's immense cultural and historic importance.

Past Kofukuji is the original wing of the **Nara National Museum** (50 Noboriojicho; Tel. (0742) 22-7771; open 9am–4:30pm daily except Mondays), linked by an underground passage to a newer, tile-roofed building just beyond it. This museum of ancient art focuses on Buddhist statues and sculptural styles from around 600 through the Middle Ages. The permanent collection is housed in the old wing, and its fascinating

> Proverb: "See Nara and die" — only when you've seen and experienced Nara can you die content.

exhibits showcase the development of Chinese-influenced Buddhist art and design. The gift shop in the underpass between the two buildings offers an excellent selection of quality souvenirs, reproductions, and posters of Nara culture.

Also on the west side of Nara Park is **Todaiji**, which—like many elaborate temple complexes—comprises many remarkable structures and artifacts. The first is the majestic Nandaimon (Great South Gate), standing over 19 m (63 ft) high and dating from 1199. Built in a classical Indian architectural style, this huge structure is only two-thirds the size of the original destroyed by a typhoon in 962. The gate houses the two Benevolent Kings, guardian deities created in the twelfth century by master sculptors Unkei and Kaikei to guard the inner temple compound.

Pass through the gate for your first view of the massive roof of the Daibutsuden straight ahead. The current building, dating from 1709, is only two-thirds the size of the original, which burned down decades earlier. On the right of the door is Binzuru, a disciple of Prince Gautama (the Buddha's original name before achieving enlightenment). His statue is said to have special healing powers; sections of the statue shine with the polish of thousands—if not millions—of hands rubbing away ailments over the centuries.Finally, inside the massive hall, deep in meditation on a massive podium within a ring of giant lotus leaves, is Nara's celebrated **Daibutsu**, or Great Buddha. Nearly 15 m (48.5 ft) tall, the gigantic cast-bronze statue is shorter than the original unveiled in 752, when it was covered in gold leaf. As with all Buddha images, the positions of the hands are highly significant. The Great Buddha's right hand is bestowing spiritual tranquillity, while the left symbolizes the granting of wishes. Seated on one side is the Nyorin Kannon, in whose hand is a jewel used to answer prayers and grant wishes; on the other is Kokuzo, who embodies wisdom and happiness.

To the east is **Nigatsu-do** (Second Month Hall), one of Todaiji's most famous subtemples, whose front portion rests on a vast network of wooden beams. The covered northern staircase and the broad stone southern staircase both lead up to the main walkway encircling the temple, which has massive lanterns and a strange assortment of artwork donated by supporting companies. Nigatsu-do hosts a spectacular fire purification festival in the second month of the lunar calendar (hence its name): the O-mizu Torii, or Water-Drawing Festival. Every night for two weeks, temple priests brandish long poles each with a flaming cedar ball at the end. They run along the front of the verandah, deliberately showering the large crowd below with burning embers that are believed to bring good luck for the coming year, burning away transgressions from the previous one. In long-exposure photographs, the entire temple appears to be on fire.

Along the foot of Mt. Wakakusa is the **Kasuga Grand Shrine**, established to house the Shinto deities of the powerful Fujiwara family. It has been a place of worship for both emperors and aristocrats for centuries. The main approach from the east (from Kofukuji temple) is lined with thousands of stone lanterns set amid lush greenery. These are illuminated in dramatic crowd-drawing cere-

Part of the Kasuga Grand Shrine in Nara—for centuries a place of worship for emperors and aristocrats alike.

monies held in early February and mid-August every year. The shrine's renowned Treasure House is one of the newest structures here, with wooden plaques in the shape of rice paddles reflecting the importance of rice in Shinto—and, by definition, Japanese—culture. A rice-planting ceremony is held in mid-March, during which the shrine's sacred rice field is symbolically replanted.

Outside Nara

South and west of modern Nara is an ancient area called Nishi-nokyo (meaning "west of the capital"), where you will find three important temples.

The sunset reflection of the twin pagodas of **Yakushiji** in a nearby lake is one of Japan's most striking and visually poetic images. Of the original buildings, only the To-to (East Pagoda) remains, considered by many to be Japan's most beautiful pagoda. Although it appears to have six stories, the pagoda is actually a three-story structure, each level having an extra roof for added visual impact. The vermilion Sai-to (West Pagoda) was built in 1980 on the site of the long-destroyed original. Between them is the Kondo (golden, or main, hall), reconstructed in 1975. Among its many notable bronze images is the Yakushi triad, comprising three blackened-bronze images: the Yakushi Buddha (dedicated to healing and medicine) seated on a medicine chest between Bodhisattvas of the sun and moon.

A ten-minute walk to the north is **Toshodaiji**, which boasts rare examples of ancient architecture and sculpture. Less spectacular than its expensively restored neighbor to the south, Toshodaiji nevertheless is the largest remaining example of Nara period architecture. Of its numerous period sculptures, the most celebrated is a 5-m (16.5-ft) thousand-armed Kannon statue.

Every culture has a single historical hero, a visionary credited with planting the seeds from which cultural, aesthetic, and ethical values flourished. For Japan, that person is the revered Prince Shotoku, early champion of Buddhism. Not only did this highly progressive leader produce Japan's first written constitution and legal code, thus laying the foundations of an organized state, he is also credited with having introduced the concept of *wa* ("harmony") as the fundamental value shaping the Japanese character. His life and achievements are celebrated at **Horyuji**, a large temple complex in southern Nara comprising forty buildings that became Japan's first UNESCO World Heritage Site. Horyuji was actually built decades after Prince Shotoku's death in 622. However, it

The newest of Yakushiji's twin pagodas, dramatically lit up at night.

The great bell of Todaiji in Nara Park. Todaiji, like many elaborate temple complexes, boasts many remarkable structures and artifacts.

stands on the site of one of Japan's earliest Buddhist temples, which he built.

After entering through the Nandaimon (Great South Gate), walk down another long walkway to the Chumon (Central Gate) and the inner temple grounds. Just past the fearsome Guardian Kings on watch for intruding evil, is the Sai-in, the western compound. This contains Horyuji's five-storied pagoda and the Kondo (main hall), built around 670 and the world's oldest wooden building. Within the To-in (eastern compound) is the octagonal Yumedono (Hall of Dreams), whose exquisite Guze Kannon statue was considered so sacred that it was completely hidden from human eyes from its dedication in 737 until 1884, when it was unwrapped by a visiting American art scholar—with the Meiji government's blessing, of course.

Also in the eastern compound is the Daihozoden (Great Treasure Hall), housing Horyuji's magnificent collection of Buddhist art, among Japan's finest. Included are over 10,000 items, 1,780 of which are classified as national treasures or important cultural assets. Highlights include an Indian-style Shaka triad; the Yumechigae ("Dream Changing") Kannon, said to transform its worshippers' nightmares into pleasant dreams; and the Kudara Kannon, a graceful, willowy statue named after a region in Korea, whose designer and creator was almost certainly Korean. Horyuji was built by craftsmen imported from Korea, and the temple bears much of their distinctive artistic stamp.

Surprisingly, Horyuji also contains a building dedicated to a foreigner: Langdon Warner, a Harvard art professor whom the Japanese have mistakenly credited with saving both Nara and Kyoto from aerial bombing during World War II. The decision to spare them was

The Roots of Japanese Culture

Nara is considered by many to be home to the very roots of Japanese culture and one of the cornerstones of Japan's unique forms of Buddhism.

Present-day Nara began life in 710 as Heijo-kyo, meaning "Citadel of Peace". Originally a flat, nondescript tract of farmland in the Yamato Plain, it was selected as the site for a new imperial capital by the Emperor Mommu, just before his early death, and by Fujiwara-no-Fuhito, the head of the powerful aristocratic Fujiwara clan and father-in law of the succeeding emperor, Shomu.

At the height of its glory, Heijo-kyo's skyline was punctuated by 50 pagodas, together with numerous temples, mansions, and the imposing imperial court itself. Despite serving as Japan's imperial capital for only 74 years, Nara's influence on Japan's cultural development has loomed large throughout the city's 1,300-year history.

actually taken by Henry Stimson, the US Secretary of War, who knew the cities from his own pre-war visits.

Osaka

More than just Japan's second city, **Osaka** is also the perfect base from which to explore nearby Nara and Kyoto by train. Although Osaka is overshadowed by Tokyo in the big-city stakes, it is a vibrant and energetic world capital in its own right and certainly has plenty to offer the curious visitor.

Indeed, for many visitors Osaka is more truly "Japanese" than Tokyo, having a more distinctive flavor and character than its sprawling rival to the east. Osakans pride themselves on being warmer, friendlier, and more spontaneous than their Tokyo cousins, whom they love to dismiss as formal and uptight. They are also renowned throughout Japan for two things: doing business and eating.

Here, business and pleasure are inextricably linked—and have been for hundreds of years. The city's commercial reputation re-

---

Osaka Museums

Osaka Castle Osaka located in Castle Park (Osaka-jo Koen), Tanamachi 4-chome; Tel. (06) 6941-3044. Open 9am–5pm daily. Admission ¥500.

Museum of Oriental Ceramics located in Nakanoshima Park; Tel. (06) 6223-0055. Open 9:30am–5pm daily except Mondays. Admission ¥500.

Kaiyukan Aquarium located in Tempozan Harbor Village; Tel. (06) 6576-5501. Open 10am–8pm daily. Admission ¥2,000 (adults), ¥900 (students/children), ¥400 (toddlers).

Osaka Municipal Museum of Art located in Tennoji Park, 1-82 Chausuyamacho, Tennoji-ku; Tel. (06) 6771-4874. Open 9:30pm–5pm daily except Mondays. Admission ¥300.

---

flects its origins as the national merchants' capital and a major trading hub. When Hideyoshi built his main castle in the center of Osaka after unifying the country in 1583, the city's prosperity seemed written in stone. With an uninhibited merchant class eager to throw its newly acquired wealth around, Osaka quickly became Japan's undisputed entertainment and theatrical center.

Despite the economic slowdown and recession of the 1990s that followed the bursting of Japan's economic bubble, anyone strolling around central Osaka's famous nighttime entertainment districts will quickly realize how much its residents love to eat, drink, and party. In fact, so dedicated are Osakans to the cult of eating that they are known for *kuidare* (eating until you drop or until you go bankrupt, depending on the interpretation).

Osaka will win no urban beauty contests, but there are plenty of sights to see here, including a couple of interesting museums, a remarkable aquarium, and an underground shopping complex that might be the world's largest.

The best way to see Osaka is by subway. Taxis are expensive and vulnerable to the city's sticky traffic situation; and information on the tourist-unfriendly bus service is almost entirely in Japanese only. An all-day subway pass (available at any ticket machine) costs the equivalent of less than four central-area subway tickets (about US$7).

A good place to start exploring is the bustling **Umeda** area, containing Japan Railways Osaka Station, three subway stations, and two private railway stations. It also has most famous department stores outside Tokyo, the gigantic Hankyu and Hanshin buildings (whose private railways serve Kyoto and Kobe). The Osaka City Tourist Information Office is just inside the main entrance to the Hankyu station. Umeda marks the northern end of the business and entertainment district popularly known as Kita (meaning simply "North"), and is the very essence of modern Osaka's hustle and bustle.

At rush hour, Umeda's teeming subway platforms rival the crowd scenes for which Tokyo's subway is so notorious. Equally impressive crowd scenes occur below Umeda in a mammoth network of shops, bars, and cozy inexpensive restaurants whose scale boggles the mind. The basement of every large building in a one-mile radius is linked to form a modern commercial labyrinth. It actually comprises several shopping centers seamlessly interconnected to ensure maximum customer and cash turnover. To explore its fascinating subterranean sights, start with the "Whity Umeda," under the Hankyu and Hanshin buildings, then move on to "Herbis Plaza"—but don't expect to see daylight again for some time.

A suitable cure for your extended period underground is to go up —40 stories up to the top of **Shin-Umeda Sky Building**. This futuristic and unusual structure is actually two glass-and-steel towers linked at the top, from which the "Floating Observatory" provides a panoramic view of Osaka city and the surrounding countryside.

Shopping arcades are a staple feature of every Japanese city, town, and village. Unsurprisingly, Osaka boasts some of Japan's most impressive—or excessive, depending on your taste. You can spend fascinating hours exploring the covered Hankyu Higashi-dori arcade near the Hankyu stations, less

Osaka truly comes alive at night, when its vibrance and sense of fun are best revealed.

upmarket but no less fascinating than the more famous Shinsaibashi arcade (see below). In the south of Kita, across from the US Consulate, is Kita Shinchi, Osaka's premiere dining and entertainment quarter, centered around the main street of Shinchi Hondori. This area is great for people-watching, but to eat here it helps to have a generous expense account.

The **Mint** is situated on the west bank of the Dojima River (opposite Sakuranomiya Park). Although its museum has a large exhibition of the history of Japanese and foreign money, it is best known for its long avenue of magnificent late-blooming cherry trees, the city's finest.

Osaka Castle stands testament to its own turbulent history—it's been built, destroyed, and rebuilt for centuries.

Just to the east of Sakuranomiya Park is the **Fujita Art Museum**, which has a fine collection of Chinese and Japanese paintings from the 11th century to the present. If you've become an adept of the tea ceremony, you'll appreciate the excellent collection of 14th-century objects: ceramic tea bowls, tea kettles, and caddies, aś well as bamboo spoons, whisks, and flower vases.

For more ceramics, stop in at the **Museum of Oriental Ceramics**, located in the garden at one end of Nakanoshima, the "central island" in the middle of the large river running through Osaka's center. Here you can find fine specimens of the Korean and Chinese ceramics that so strongly influenced Japan's own styles. Most of Osaka's municipal buildings are on Nakanoshima, including an elegant European-style town hall dating from 1918, one of the few red-brick buildings in Japan.

Here you'll also get a splendid view of **Osaka Castle**, which is dramatically illuminated at night. To celebrate his unification of Japan after more than a century of civil war, Hideyoshi had made the castle the country's greatest fortress, so the Tokugawa felt obliged to destroy it in 1615 after snatching power away from Hideyoshi's heir. They later rebuilt it to bolster their own prestige, only to burn it down once again in a fit of pique when the Meiji Restoration of imperial power abolished their shogunate in 1868. Today, a reinforced-concrete replica reproduces only the great five-storied tower, 42 m (138 ft) high, surrounded by moats and ivy-covered ramparts. The castle contains an interesting but disappointingly modern museum displaying armor, weapons, costumes, and historical documents. There's also an enchanting collection of *bunraku* puppets—a rare chance to see them at close range.

Providing a welcome touch of green amid all the asphalt, ginkgo and sycamore trees line the impressive Midosuji Boulevard. This thoroughfare runs south from Umeda to Kita's southern counterpart, Minami. On one side of Midosuji is America-mura, the favorite posing ground for Osaka's desperately trendy youth, so named for the large number of stores selling much-sought-after secondhand apparel imported from the US.

One block east of Midosuji is Osaka's famous **Shinsaibashi shopping arcade**, a consumer-frenzy mecca second in national status only to Ginza and Shinjuku in Tokyo. If you have time for only one evening walk in Osaka, this is the one. Although the arcade begins over a mile north, start from exit 6 of Shinsaibashi Station on the Midosuji subway line, between the Sogo and Daimaru department stores, and turn right to make your way south.

Every night of the week, this entire area is teeming with business-man frequenting night clubs, hostess bars, and private drinking clubs. (Many of these clubs are confusingly called "snack bars." But tourists beware! These bizarre establishments are the true home of the $20 glass of beer, with prices aimed squarely at lonely executives with expense accounts looking for a home away from home.)

This is where Osaka's trendy youth prowl for action, as do many of Osaka's growing pack of young foreign residents seduced by the lure of easy yen. On Saturday afternoons and evenings, the place is a teeming throng of humanity. Wandering the side streets at night allows you to soak up the heady atmosphere of pleasure and commerce that has characterized this part of Osaka for centuries.

At the far south is the small Ebisu Bridge, a favorite meeting place for Osaka's trendiest young things. Just before you cross the bridge, on your left is an arch announcing the start of **Soemon-cho**, a colorful street of late-night restaurants and night clubs that is Minami's answer to Kita-Shinchi near Umeda. Note the ultra-modern black-and-chrome Kirin Plaza beer hall next to the entrance to bustling Soemon-cho.

As you cross the bridge, stop in the middle to immerse yourself in the sights and sounds of the people, the blazing neon, and the Dotomburi River below you. Hundreds of years ago, in Osaka's heyday as the country's theater and entertainment capital, the biggest stars would arrive by boat to enter the riverside back entrances of the many theaters on Dotomburi, which is just south of the river. Frenzied fans would pack this very bridge for a glimpse of their idols arriving in ornate medieval waterborne equivalents of the modern stretch limousine.

Turning left on the other side of the bridge brings you to **Dotomburi**, which at night is Osaka's ultimate assault on the senses. A cornucopia of bizarre creatures adorn the buildings flanking this pedestrian mall: giant monsters slither down the buildings, restaurants, cine-

The consumer's mecca: Shinsaibashi's famous shopping arcade draws flocks of spenders—and people-watchers.

Along Osaka's "Kitchen Street," assorted Japanese bric-a-brac—such as these paper lanterns—make ideal souvenirs.

mas, theaters, games centers, and steamy noodle bars. No photograph can capture the intensity of this strange and unforgettable concourse.

At the other end of Dotomburi is the Nipponbashi area. This is where you will find Den-Den Town, Osaka's sadly underwhelming answer to Tokyo's Akihabara electronics district. Nipponbashi is also famous as the national home of *bunraku,* Japan's dazzling traditional puppet theater. Although various forms of puppet theater date back to the 11th century, the remarkably expressive and elaborately costumed bunraku style was thriving by the 17th century in both Osaka and Kyoto. Although its popularity waned during the Meiji period, it has been "rediscovered" this century, the most dramatic evidence being the vast investment in the **National Bunraku Theater** in Nipponbashi.

Bunraku is a Japanese performance art of surprising dramatic intensity, worth seeing if only for an hour or so in the middle of a busy day of sightseeing. Although all dialog and narration are in Japanese, an English interpretation device or an English program is always available. Many of the most popular heroic and tragic dramas were written by Osaka's own Monzaemon Chikamatsu (1653–1724), the playwright the Japanese claim as their own Shakespeare.

In the neighboring Namba district, the **Shin-Kabuki-za Theater** (at the bottom of Midosuji Boulevard) gives *kabuki* performances only three weeks each year. But there's plenty of other traditional drama such as *kyogen* farces and *manzai* comic double-acts. In spring, the Osaka International Festival of drama and music takes place both at the theater and in the Festival Hall on Nakanoshima Island. Even if you don't bother venturing within, the building itself is dramatic and should not be missed.

Between the Nipponbashi and Namba districts, try to find nearby Doguya-suji, ("Kitchen Street"), a narrow alley of restaurant wholesalers. This is the place to buy souvenirs of all the imitation food you've seen in restaurant windows, together with Japanese-style plates, bowls, glasses, sake sets, lacquerware, giant paper lanterns, and a million other things you never expected to see for sale.

South of Namba, between Ebisucho and Tennoji stations, is the Tsutenkaku Tower, a rather desperate imitation of the Eiffel Tower (and perhaps the only structure that makes Kyoto's tower look impressive). The view from the observation deck over 300 ft up is panoramic but hardly worth the effort.

The nearby **Osaka Municipal Art Museum**, near Tennoji Station, is worth visiting for its celebrated Abe Collection of 200 Chinese paintings (ninth–13th centuries) and its Ming- and Ching-dynasty ceramics (14th–19th centuries). The large permanent encampment of homeless people around Tennoji Park makes the area more than a little seedy (but not at all dangerous).

Close by is Osaka's most famous temple, **Shitennoji**, founded in 593 by the revered reforming lawgiver, Prince Shotoku. Unfortunately, the buildings in this large temple are concrete reproductions of the

originals destroyed by bombing in World War II. However, the large stone torii gateway is the oldest in Japan, dating back to 1294. Shitennoji also hosts Osaka's largest temple market on the 21st of each month, featuring antiques, used clothing, and miscellaneous items.

Farther south is the **Sumiyoshi Taisha** shrine, dedicated to the god of peace, song, and seafaring. The shrine's large and attractive arched bridge is just one of the features enjoyed by the three million visitors who come to make prayer offerings on the first three days of the New Year. Although the shrine is thought to have been founded in the third century, the present buildings are relatively recent reproductions.

Finally, Osaka Port at the far west of the city offers two ideal distractions for all the family. The futuristic **Kaiyukan Aquarium** has at its core one of the world's largest indoor tanks,

Carnivore's delight: Kobe beef, the city's most famous product, has a strong, unique flavor.

containing a dramatic collection of sharks and other large deep-sea fish. Arranged in a descending spiral around it are other tanks representing the denizens of the Pacific Ocean's seismic "ring of fire."

The aquarium is set in a large complex of unusual shops and restaurants that also contains the **Suntory Museum**. In addition to regular art exhibitions, this wildly abstract structure features Osaka's IMAX wide-screen theater. The entire area makes for a great afternoon's break from the pressures of Osaka sightseeing.

Kobe

Kobe exploded onto the world's headlines with the suddenness of the earthquake that ravaged the city 17 January 1995, claiming a final death toll of over 6,000. But a combination of remarkable communal solidarity and determination coupled with extensive private- and public-sector investment lie behind a recovery that is nothing short of astonishing.

Hemmed in into a narrow coastal strip between the Rokko Mountains and the Inland Sea, this port city came into its own after American pressure forced Japan to open to foreign trade in 1868. The merchants who established a foothold in Kobe included large numbers of Persians and Indian traders. Today it is still known within Japan for its small but highly visible foreign business community, some of whose families have called Kobe home for generations. Kobe is a major cosmopolitan center with thriving restaurants, bars, and nightlife, not to mention Nankin-machi, Japan's most famous "Chinatown."

One early influence of the foreign residents was the development of the nationally famous Kobe beef in a country that had never touched the stuff until foreign barbarians began demanding steaks. Although meat eating is now considered commonplace, it is still strongly associated with the cosmopolitan, "Western" lifestyle that has such all-pervasive appeal in modern Japanese society. Raised nearby in Tajima or Tamba, the cattle produce a uniquely fatty meat, with a special flavor said to come from a daily dose of strong beer.

The price in the restaurants on Tor Road is exorbitant, but you might like to try the beef either grilled straight or prepared Japanese-style as *sashimi* (raw), *sukiyaki* (thinly sliced and pan-fried), or *shabu-shabu* (stewed in a hot-pot broth).

Kobe's two main downtown shopping districts are Sannomiya and neighboring Motomachi, both featuring large department stores and fashionable boutiques. Numerous smaller shops are in the Kokashita arcade, a long but narrow covered shopping passage beneath the JR tracks that is definitely not for the claustrophobic.

Kobe's biggest tourist draw, though, is mainly of interest to domestic Japanese visitors. **Kitano**, the old foreign merchants' residential district, preserves some of the 19th-century European-style houses that survived World War II. For foreign tourists, the most interesting thing about this area will probably be witnessing the fascination these residences hold over Japanese visitors. Kitano's Hindu temple, mosque, and synagogue add to the exotic appeal of this unusual area.

Dominating the mountain range that provides Kobe's dramatic backdrop is **Mt. Rokko**, which offers a wide range of natural and man-made attractions To escape the stifling heat of summer, everyone except the super-fit takes the ten-minute cable car ride to the top. Here you will discover a commanding view of Kobe, Osaka, Awaji Island, and the Inland Sea. The many hiking and cycling trails draw nature-lovers throughout the year.

Behind Mt. Rokko is **Arima Onsen**, one of Japan's oldest hot-spring resorts. Like popular hot-spring resorts around the country, this small town has been the site of furious development, and the many small traditional inns *(ryokan)* and bathhouses are now dwarfed by large, ugly concrete hotels. Nevertheless, Arima Onsen still offers an ideal introduction to the pleasures of bathing Japanese-style, whether through a visit of a few hours to one of the large and luxuriously equipped centers, or a night spent in a traditional family-run hot-spring inn.

☞ Ise-Shima

Ise-Shima National Park, southeast of Osaka, is home to the Outer and Inner shrines of Ise. These deceptively simple structures are no less than the sacred repository of the national identity—Shinto sanctuaries dedicated nearly 2,000 years ago to Japan's founding deities. Their atmospheric setting in serene woodland reveals more strongly than anywhere else the profound links between modern Japan and its mythical origins. Be forewarned: for foreign tourists, Ise is not a destination for picturesque sightseeing, and there isn't really very much to see or photograph (especially since taking pictures of the Inner Shrine is forbidden). Rather, it provides an opportunity to glimpse one key aspect of the very essence of a society and people whose origins, development, and identity hold a fascination for the rest of the world.

Shinto shrines are found throughout Japan, and reflect key elements of the national identity.

While no more nor less significant than other countries' national symbols and icons, the Shinto identity embodied in the shrines of Ise is quite distinct from Japan's other man-made institutions. Nature itself is the primal essence enshrined and worshipped at Ise, as implied by the carefully orchestrated approach to the sanctuaries past the limpid Isuzu River and through the forest. Although the sacred structures represent the ultimate focus of the Shinto religion, they are dismantled and renewed every 20 years—one of the most explicit manifestations of the traditional Japanese belief in transience and perpetual renewal.

Both the Inner and Outer shrines comprise a main hall and two treasure houses, each enclosed within four fences. Only members of the imperial family and high-ranking priests are allowed past the second of the four fences. This restriction reinforces the notion of the imperial family as living descendents and representatives of the gods—despite the emperor's renunciation of divinity announced as one of the terms of surrender at the end of World War II (when some people literally fainted upon hearing the emperor's voice on the radio for the first time). Indeed, so sacred are the Ise shrines that, despite the relatively peaceful coexistence of Shinto and Buddhism in Japan, Buddhist monks and nuns were banned from entering the precincts prior to the Meiji Restoration of 1868.

The shrines are most easily reached from Nagoya via the Kintetsu Railway to Uji-Yamada Station. In addition to the famous shrines, you can explore more of this attractively scenic peninsula, with its national park, the haunting image of the sacred "wedded rocks" at Futamigaura beach, and the resort town of Kashikojima at the southern end of the Kintetsu railway's Shima line.

The Outer Shrine

A short walk from Uji-Yamada Station is **Geku**, the Outer Shrine. It is dedicated to the God of the Earth, who was sent down to Japan by the Sun Goddess Amaterasu. Originally situated near present-day Kyoto, the shrine was moved here in 478. The main entrance takes you to the first sacred gateway (torii), which in Japan always symbolizes the threshold of holy ground. Both shrines' surprisingly primitive design is thought to be based on those of granaries and storehouses from prehistoric times.

As you walk along the avenue of pines and giant cedars, you pass on the right the Anzaisho, the emperor's rest house, and Sanshujo, the rest house for the imperial family. Beyond a second *torii* is the Kaguraden, Hall of the Sacred Dances. In return for a donation to the shrine, the shrine maidens *(miko)*, dressed in the typically Shinto outfit of bright-red pleated skirts with white blouses, will perform one of the dances. The girls wield branches of the holy *sakaki* tree and dance to an orchestra composed of wooden clappers *(hyoshigi)*, plucked zither *(koto)*, mouth organ *(sho)*, and the oboe-like *hichiriki*, together with flute and drum.

The avenue ends at the Geku's Shoden (main shrine building), which—together with its eastern and western treasure houses—is enclosed by a series of four unvarnished wooden fences. This is where Shinto priests in white robes with black belts and black lacquered clogs stand to bless worshippers as they make a silent obeisance. The Shoden itself is just 6 m (20 ft) high, a little less in width, and 10 m (33 ft) long.

Each shrine is constructed of plain, unadorned Japanese cypress wood, brought especially from the Kiso Mountains in the Central Alps, northeast of Nagoya. The style of the cross-beamed roofs and simple wooden frames is the same as that used more than 2,000 years ago, before Chinese architecture exerted its influence when Buddhism arrived here from Korea. This is a special style of Shinto architecture that is prohibited from being used at other shrines.

Concern for ritual purification requires that Japanese pilgrims rinse their mouths at a water trough when approaching a shrine. Priests wave sacred branches over the faithful.

The **Geku-Jin-en Sacred Park**, at the foot of Mt. Takakura, is an integral part of the sanctuary and a beautiful place for a quiet stroll. In fact, if you don't feel like taking the bus, the walk to the inner shrine takes you along a delightful tree-shaded avenue lined with stone lanterns.

The Inner Shrine

The **Naiku** (Inner Shrine) is the more important of the two shrines, as it is dedicated to Amaterasu, the Sun Goddess and supreme deity

Mizumejizo-san statues on display at Okunoin, Japan's most famous cemetery.

of Shinto. The Naiku holds the sacred eight-pointed mirror *(yata-no-kagami)*, which is one of the three symbols of the imperial throne. (The others are the sword, which resides at the Atsuta Shrine in Nagoya, and the jewel, kept in the Imperial Palace in Tokyo.) The Naiku's layout and the construction of its Shoden are similar to those of the Geku, although the approach to the Naiku over the Uji Bridge across the Isuzu River is more picturesque. Like the shrines, the bridge is renewed every two decades.

The ritual dismantling of the shrines every 20 years (known as *sengu-shiki*) goes back to prehistoric times, when sacred structures tended to be erected for special ceremonies rather than as permanent places of worship. You will notice beside each shrine an area of open ground on which the new shrine is to be erected—in 2013—in identical form. The structures are broken up into small pieces and distributed to the faithful as talismans. The whole process is both painstaking and expensive, and the "democratization" of the imperial institutions since the emperor renounced his divinity means the shrines (rather than the state) must now foot the bill. To defray costs, worshippers must make a generous donation to receive a piece of the old shrine.

You can join the Japanese visitors down at the Isuzu River, where they perform a rite of purification by washing their mouths with its clear, fresh waters. At the same time, they play with the fat red, silver, and black carp swimming around nearby.

Wakayama

South of Osaka is **Wakayama**, a large prefecture whose long coastline and lush greenery have long been a magnet for domestic tourists. In addition to hundreds of temples, shrines, and hot-spring resorts, Wakayama features some of the country's most popular beaches.

Farther south is **Koyasan**, the center of the Shingon branch of esoteric Buddhism and one of Japan's most important religious enclaves. Now comprising over 120 temple buildings as well as numerous shrines, pagodas, and stupas, this large religious settlement is located at the top of Mt. Koya, a 1,006-m (3,300-ft) peak. Koyasan was already known as a sacred site for ascetic practices when Kobo Daishi, a revered Buddhist priest, teacher, and scholar, received imperial permission to establish a religious community to develop his new Shingon sect in 816.

The mausoleum of the *kukai* ("great teacher," as he is known) is located at the deepest reaches of **Okunoin**, Japan's most famous cemetery and one of Koyasan's biggest draws. Once the kukai was buried there, the great and the humble alike were quick to see the merit of a final resting place near the great teacher. The graves of hundreds of thousands from all walks of life now occupy the site, with the remains of emperors, warlords, warriors, samurai, and poets all jostling for space. Their tombs and stone markers range from the ostentatious to the elegant, the well preserved to the decrepit.

Well over a million ancestor-worshipping Japanese descend on Koyasan and Okunoin on major public holidays, especially those commemorating the dead. If you are wise enough to avoid these times, consider spending the night in one of some 60 temple lodgings *(shukubo)* that offer surprisingly comfortable traditional accommodation to visitors and travelers. The main highlight of a stay at one of these special temples is the chance to sample the luxurious Buddhist vegetarian temple cuisine *(shojin-ryori)* served only in such lodgings. The path to enlightenment can indeed be surprisingly pleasurable.

CHUBU

The central region of Honshu (Japan's main island), **Chubu** stretches northeast from Kansai across the Hida, Kiso, and Akaishi mountains—known collectively as the Japan Alps—to the plains of the north coast and the Sea of Japan. It's most easily explored in an excursion from the Kansai region by train in a picturesque mountain-railroad journey from Nagoya. You can visit the charming town of Takayama, set in the midst of imposing mountain scenery, and the historical city of Kanazawa.

☞ Takayama

The Takayama-line train, from Nagoya via Gifu, takes you along the Kiso and Hida river valleys. The leisurely three-hour ride passes through steep gorges, narrow terraced rice paddies, and neatly tailored tea plantations hugging the mountain slopes with not a square inch of usable land wasted. The train stops by riverside markets where farmers trade fruit, vegetables, and gossip with passengers.

Takayama is a town famous for its carpenters—a reputation going back to the great days of the imperial courts of Nara and Kyoto. With the harvests of its Hida mountain district too meager to contribute taxes to the national treasury, the town sent instead its skillful artisans *(Hida no takumi)* to help build the temples and palaces of the imperial capital. Those skills have been handed down to present-day craftsmen working in yew wood, and the old timbered houses are exquisitely maintained in traditional style. The local lord in turn borrowed the capital's grid pattern when laying out medieval Takayama, which became known as "Little Kyoto."

Just as Kyoto offers some of the most splendid traditional inns *(ryokan),* so Takayama is a good place to try out family-style guesthouses

An elderly Takayama resident looks on. Takayamans are famous for their carpentry and exquisite woodcarvings, laquerware, and pottery.

(*minshuku;* see page 229)—they're especially friendly here. All you need to get around are your own two feet, although renting a bicycle at the railway station will give you easy access to the surrounding countryside.

Start your day at the open-air Asaichi morning market down on the east bank of the Miya River, north of Yasugawa Street bridge. Savor the clear mountain air as you enjoy the display of fruit and vegetables from Hida farms and the flowers and nuts brought down from the hills.

A little way back from the river, heading south, you'll find the delightful old houses and workshops of Kami-Sannomachi and Furuimachinami streets. The high-quality craftwork here—woodcarvings, laquerware, and pottery—is renowned throughout Japan. Furuimachinami is quieter and more residential, with long, two-story, unpainted dark timber houses, lattice façades, and low-balconied verandahs, plus a few flowers and shrubs in pots or *hako-*

niwa box gardens to add some color. Some of the old houses have been redeveloped as museums and eclectic galleries.

Just east of the riverside market are two merchants' houses, Yoshijima-ke and Kusakabe Mingeikan, the latter turned into a superb folkcraft museum displaying local costumes, woodcarvings, and the fine, transparent lacquerware *(shunkeinuri)* that highlights rather than conceals the grain of the wood.

Takayama's most important temple is 16th-century **Kokubunji**. Next to the three-story pagoda is a ginkgo tree said to be over 1,000 years old. Southeast of town is Shiroyama Park, whose unlandscaped slopes covered with wildflowers have a pleasantly natural look and offer an extensive panorama of the town and the Japan Alps beyond.

Hida Minzoku-Mura is a fascinating open-air museum of authentic old farmhouses from the region, most of them rescued from an area flooded by nearby Mihoro Dam. Laid out in an attractive hillside setting half a mile southwest of Takayama Station, the houses—many of them three or four stories high, with steeply pitched grass-thatch roofs—are oddly reminiscent of those in European Alpine villages. The houses display old farm tools and cooking utensils, and some operate as workshops where you can watch the much-vaunted local craftsmen demonstrating their skills in lacquerwork, carving, weaving, and dyeing.

Hikers and mountain climbers won't want to miss the bus excursion (95 minutes from Takayama) to **Nori-kura**, a 3,026-m (9,928-ft) volcano at the southern end of Japan Alps National Park. For the hikers, a bus goes to a point quite close to the summit, after which it's an easy but exhilarating walk to the top.

Kanazawa

The largest city in northern Chubu, **Kanazawa** has been able to preserve its older charms from the assaults of the Tokugawa shoguns and the bombs of World War II by pursuing a peaceful career of arts, crafts, and scholarship. It is home to a major university as well as an arts and crafts college. Kanazawa is still considered an archetypal castle town, even though the university now occupies the spot once dominated by the long-destroyed castle. Still, there are some very pleasant walks around what are still referred to as the castle grounds.

Kenrokuen Park, a classical Edo-period "strolling" garden regarded as one of the three best in Japan, is a good place to start your visit. The park has a plethora of ponds spanned by elegant stone bridges, together with stone lanterns, waterfalls, serpentine streams, cherry trees, and pines. Artfully constructed hillocks provide panoramic views of the landscaping. The central Kasumigaike (Misty Lake) is the most attractive of the ponds, graced by its Tortoise Shell Island—the tortoise being much favored by the Japanese as a symbol of long life.

> A Japanese garden is like a painter's canvas: trees, rocks, plants, and water serve as elements of texture, color, perspective, and spatial relationships.

Among Kanazawa's other specialties is its pretty five-color glazed *kutani* pottery, which you'll see in many downtown shops. If you're interested enough to make a small investment, first look at the marvelous samples in the Municipal Art Museum in the park before buying.

West of the park is Nagamachi, the old samurai quarter. Wander freely along the secluded canals past the dark timbered houses, all situated in very narrow, zigzagging streets to hamper enemy attack. The superb **Saihitsu-an** house features silk-dyers creating unbelievably expensive material for kimono.

On the eastern edge of town, north of the Umeno Hashi bridge across the Asano River, is the old geisha district, slightly more run-down than Nagamachi but no less quaint.

WESTERN HONSHU AND SHIKOKU

The area around the Inland Sea offers a wide range of attractions, from the varied towns and cities of Western Honshu to the major pilgrimage destination of Shikoku island.

☛ Himeji

Himeji's magnificent castle is unquestionably one of the region's "must-do" sights. As Japan's only surviving castle preserved in its original form, **Himeji Castle** has opulent white walls and myriad turrets. These have earned it the nickname Shirasagi ("White Heron Castle") for the way its swooping, white-gabled profile proudly soars above this small city. The castle dates from the early 1600s. When the famous unifiers Nobunaga, Hideyoshi, and Tokugawa fought to end the 16th-century civil wars, Hideyoshi used Himeji as a base of operations against the recalcitrant warlords of Western Honshu. Although much of the castle's interior seems dark and aus-

A magical night view of Himeji's splendid castle—the only castle in Japan still preserved in its original form.

tere, this highlights the magnificent wood floors and paneling and the superb joinery and construction techniques.

A special combination ticket is available for both Himeji Castle and nearby **Koko-en**, a superb landscaped garden built in 1992 by a Kyoto based master gardener on the site of a former samurai residence. Koko-en actually comprises nine distinct gardens, each with a special theme such as bamboo, pine trees, seedlings, summer trees, and flowers. Don't miss the tea ceremony garden, carefully designed to be appreciated from the traditional Urasenke-style teahouse, where visitors (and especially foreign tourists) are invited to relax on *tatami* mats and enjoy a bowl of strong green tea and a sweet ceremoniously served by elegant kimono-clad tea ceremony students. (When served your bowl of tea, don't forget to bow slowly and turn the tea bowl three times before sipping the frothy brew.)

Kurashiki

Surrounded by heavily industrialized suburbs, the old center of **Kurashiki** has canals lined with dreamy willow trees—a reverse comment on the horrors of war. This is practically the only town of any consequence here along the Inland Sea coast to have emerged unscathed from the terrible fire-bombings of 1945. It thus provides an all-too-rare glimpse of provincial life in prewar Japan.

In the era of the Tokugawa shoguns, the canals were used to carry rice and grain in barges for onward shipment to the great markets of Osaka and Edo. The elegant black-brick granaries have been beautifully preserved to house the town's many museums of art, folkcrafts, and archeology. You'll certainly find a day's visit to Kurashiki a very welcome change from the relentless modernity of some of the cities nearby.

Take a short taxi ride from the station to the museum district, then do the rest on foot. There are half a dozen museums tucked into an elbow of the canal, but not all of them are worth seeing. Be sure to note down the Japanese names of the better ones before setting out.

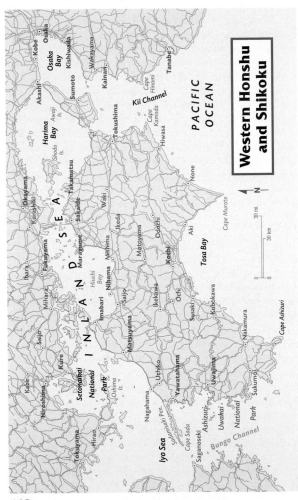

Western Honshu and Shikoku

N

PACIFIC OCEAN

Osaka · Kobe · Akashi · Osaka Bay · Kishiwada · Wakayama · Kainari · Cape Hinomi · Tanabé · Sumoto · Harima Bay · Awaji Is. · Shodo Is. · Kii Channel · Tokushima · Cape Kamoda · Hiwasa · Okayama · Kurashiki · Takamatsu · Sakaide · Waki · None · Ibara · Fukuyama · Marugame · Mishima · Ikeda · Odochi · Aki · Cape Muroto · Mihara · Hiuchi Bay · Niihama · Saijo · Motoyama · Kochi · Tosa Bay · Saijo · Imabari · Matsuyama · Ikekawa · Ochi · Susaki · Kubokawa · Kabe · Kure · INLAND SEA · Setonaikai National Park · Oshima Is. · Uchiko · Nagahama · Yawatahama · Uwajima · Nakamura · Cape Ashizuri · Hiroshima · Tokuyama · Hirao · Iyo Sea · Sdamisaki Pen. · Cape Sada · Saganoseki · Ashizuri · Uwakai National Park · Sukumo · Bungo Channel

30 mi.
30 km

148

One of the most delightful is the **Kurashiki Mingeikan** folk art museum, displaying not only Japanese, Korean, and Chinese pottery, glassware, textiles, and bamboo-ware, but also Native American and European peasant ceramics and basketry with which to compare the Asian art. The Ohara Tokikan pottery hall is devoted to the work of modern pottery masters Kanjiro Kawai, Shoji Hamada, and Kenkichi Tomimoto, as well as their much admired friend, Bernard Leach, the influential British potter credited with popularizing Japanese rustic ceramic styles and techniques abroad.

At the **Kurashiki Bijutsukan** municipal art museum, the outside world is very much the focus of the Ninagawa family's collection of ancient Greek, Egyptian, Roman, and Persian ceramics, sculpture, and mosaics, plus 19th-century French and Italian marble and bronze sculptures. There is also some astonishing Rococo porcelain from Meissen, Vienna, Berlin, and Sèvres. You'll find a completely furnished traditional Japanese living room on the fourth floor.

If you've become an enthusiast of large "strolling" gardens, the 18th-century **Korakuen**, in the nearby town of Okayama, is considered a must by connoisseurs. The Japanese have adopted the traditional Chinese practice of ranking sights and places, and Korakuen is "officially" one of Japan's three greatest gardens. At the garden's famous tea pavilion you can sample a tea ceremony while contemplating the cherry and plum trees on one side in the spring or the blazing maples on the other in autumn.

Across the Asahi River, you can see the ruins of **Okayama Castle**, unusually painted black and called Ujo ("The Crow") in deliberate contrast to Himeji's "White Heron Castle."

Hiroshima

Your first reaction as the train pulls into Hiroshima Station might well be surprise. After all, the very name "Hiroshima" has become a modern metaphor, the ultimate symbol of total obliteration. Yet around the station you see tower blocks, neon signs, cars zipping along the high-

way—all the signs of a normal town. In fact, modern **Hiroshima** is a city of broad avenues, green parks, and almost a million citizens, which is more than double its World War II population.

You might find yourself looking at an old man or woman, guessing how old they were on 6 August 1945 and trying to imagine what they were doing at 8:15am, the instant of the atomic explosion that reverberated around the world. The movingly simple **Peace Memorial Museum** documents the horror with charts, models, photographs, videos, everyday objects transformed by the unimaginable heat of the blast, and a life-sized diorama portraying horribly burned victims. One of the most powerful exhibits is a single photograph: a human shadow left imprinted on the steps of the Sumitomo Bank at the moment of the "flash."

The museum will surprise many visitors expecting a vic-

Colored paper cranes laid at the children's memorial in the Peace Park.

A Humble People

Of all the habits and characteristics the Japanese are known for, two of the most enduring are their humility and their politeness. Interpersonal relationships are still largely driven by a constant desire to achieve consensus and avoid disagreement and confrontation.

In Japan's rigidly structured hierarchical society, people's relative status needs to be established at the outset of any interaction. That is why exchanging business cards is an important preliminary to any meeting or discussion. It conveys the essential details of where you work and what your status is within that organization. (What you actually do is not considered so important.)

However, when dealing with foreigners, the Japanese instinct for warm hospitality usually comes to the fore. People are expected to adopt an outward appearance of humility, which often results in highly self-deprecating comments—especially in the presence of honored foreign guests. "Our economy is so bad." "Our houses must seem so small." "Our prices are so high."

Resist the temptation to join in the apparently masochistic highlighting of Japan's shortcomings. The intelligent tourist will quickly realize that the appropriate response is actually to disagree politely and instead find something to praise.

Thus, although the Japanese famously seek consensus and abhor having to say "No," there are times when disagreeing is highly recommended. This is especially important when responding to some of the exaggerated phrases Japanese hosts are expected to offer to regret their inadequate hospitality. For example, if you are invited to dine in a Japanese home and the arrival of your meal is accompanied by a standard apology ("This is mouth-dirtying food"), it is best to disagree politely but firmly.

tim's account of one of this century's most controversial decisions; yet the curators have gone to considerable lengths to document the horror of atomic weapons and nuclear war in general, driving toward the inevitable conclusion that such weapons must never again be used.

Outside the museum, the **Cenotaph** contains the names of the 108,956 casualties, with the inscription: "Let all the souls here rest in peace, for the evil shall not be repeated." There is also a huge bronze Peace Bell. At the northern end of the park stands the lone

Hard to believe but Iwakuni Bridge, located near Miyajima, was built without the use of a single nail!

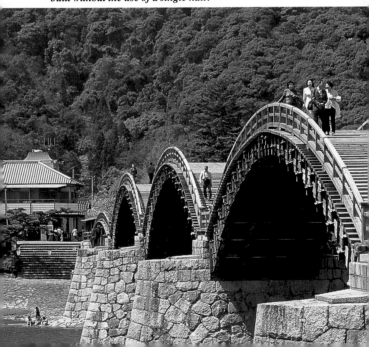

structure preserved since 1945: the former Hiroshima Prefectural Industrial Promotion Hall, now known as the "A-Bomb Dome."

After visiting the emotionally powerful museum, you may wish to seek a therapeutic antidote in the lively shopping centers east of the park around Hondori, Hachobori, and Kamiya-cho. But the ultimate venue to restore the spirit is tranquil Miyajima, just 30 minutes away.

Miyajima

Also known as Itsukushima after its celebrated waterfront shrine, **Miyajima** island is one of Japan's most popular travel destinations. Make a very early start to beat the crowds. (It takes about 25 minutes

from Hiroshima to Miyajima-guchi Station via Japan Railways, and then 10 minutes by ferry to the island.)

Even if you feel you've seen enough Japanese temples, you will certainly be moved by the striking beauty of the bright red camphor-wood arch of **Itsukushima Shrine** rising 16 m (52 ft) out of the sea in front of the low, brilliant vermilion buildings, themselves raised above the water by stilts. Founded as far back as the 6th century, the shrine is so sacred that, until the fresh wind of reforms instituted dur-

Western Honshu and Shikoku Museums

Hiroshima Peace Memorial Museum 1-3 Nakajima-cho, Naka-ku, Hiroshima; Tel. (0822) 414004. Open daily 9am–6pm (1 May–30 November), 9am–5pm (1 December–30 April). Admission ¥50.

Takamatsu Folk Art Museum 7-minute walk from Yashima Station; Tel. (0868) 433111. Open daily 8:30–5pm. Free admission.

Korakuen Garden take bus from Okayama Station; Tel. (0862) 721148. Open daily 7:30am–6pm. Admission ¥350 (adults), ¥140 (children).

Kurashiki Ohara Museum 10-minute walk from JR Kurashiki Station; Tel. (0864) 220005. Open 9am–5pm daily except Mondays. Admission ¥1,000 (adults), ¥600 (students), ¥500 (children).

Kurashiki Bijutsukan Municipal Art Museum 10-min. walk from JR Kurashiki Station; Tel. (0864) 256024. Open 9am–5pm daily except Mondays. Admission ¥200 (adults), ¥100 (students), ¥50 (children).

Kurashiki Mingeikan Museum of Folkcraft 1-4-11 Chuo-ku, Kurashiki; Tel. (0864) 221637. Open daily except Mondays 9am–4:15pm (December–February), 9am–5pm (March–November). Admission ¥500.

ing the Meiji era beginning 1868, pregnant women and the seriously ill were carried to the mainland to ensure that no births or deaths would occur on the island. Mourners had to undergo 50 days of purification before being allowed back on Miyajima. While most such religious laws have been relaxed, burials are still not permitted here.

Still, Miyajima manages to be both solemn and lively. Sacred *bugaku* and *kagura* dances are performed at the shrine, while numerous souvenir shops do a roaring trade in the local specialties: woodcarvings, both sacred and utterly pornographic, and maple-leaf-shaped sweet buns (*momiji*). You'll find handsome polished cedarwood cups, bowls, trays, and masks—as well as kitsch rendi-

> A trip to the shrine on Miyajima island provides an ideal complement to the emotionally challenging visit to nearby Hiroshima.

tions of the tame deer that loiter lazily around the island's major tourist attractions, waiting (sometimes impatiently) for a free snack from yet another fascinated visitor.

Although most people take the ropeway, the easily negotiable trail leading to the top of 530-m (1,739-ft) **Mt. Misen** is an invigorating hike. The forest is lush and, past the secluded Gumonjido Buddhist temple, the view from the top over the Inland Sea to Hiroshima is a fine reward. From the top of Mt. Misen is one of the "three finest views" in Japan.

For such a small island, Miyajima has much to offer. But stay until after the crowds depart in the late afternoon and early evening. To take in the sight of the great shrine against the glorious setting sun, spend the night at one of Miyajima's many Japanese-style hotels and inns, preferably a family-run ryokan or pension (see page 228). After dinner, don your cotton *yukata* robe and pad out the short distance back to the Itsukushima Shrine. After sundown, the shrine's atmosphere is utterly transformed—cool, dark, and more than slightly surreal, with the subtly illuminated arch dominating the scene. If the tide is out, walk down to the base of the shrine to appreciate its massive scale.

Shikoku

Despite being **Shikoku** island's largest town, **Matsuyama** is a laid-back place, mainly serving as the shopping center for tourists visiting the hot springs situated 4 km (2.5 miles) away. **Dogo Spa** is a great place to try out a public bathhouse: don your cotton kimono and clogs, too (if you can manage them). The spring water is alkaline and crystal clear, and good for stomach ailments, the lungs, and the nervous system.

Pleasingly unlandscaped, **Shiroyama Park** covers the lovely wooded slopes of Katsuyama Hill. It is dominated by the well-preserved **Matsuyama Castle**, which was once the redoubt of the Matsudaira daimyo. This most faithful lieutenant of the Tokugawa clan distinguished himself by planting the cedar forest around the shoguns' mausoleums at Nikko.

Just a mile from Dogo Spa is the 14th-century **Ishiteji** temple, one of the 88 stages of the springtime Buddhist pilgrimage around Shikoku defined by Kobo Daishi, founder of Shingon esoteric Buddhism. Notice the especially handsome Niomon Gate.

Situated at the eastern end of Shikoku, across the Inland Sea from Kurashiki and Okayama, is **Takamatsu**, another friendly provincial town where foreigners seem to receive a particularly warm welcome. The citizens are very proud of Ritsurin Park, with its bizarre twisted pines and strangely shaped boulders. The folk art museum here is worth a visit, but also stop for a gracious tea ceremony at the delightful Kiku-getsu-tei pavilion.

On the bullet train, attendants bow respectfully as they enter and exit each car. They provide snack service plus a luxurious hot towel.

Don't miss the pavilion's little rock garden, a classic of the genre.

A 20-minute tram ride takes you out to the Yashima peninsula, formerly an island famed for the momentous battles in which the Minamoto clan drove out their Taira rivals in 1182, heralding the country's rule by military dictatorship for the next seven centuries.

Today, ruins of the Taira clan's dwellings are still visible, and Yashimaji temple houses relics of the battles.

KYUSHU

Lying the farthest southwest of Japan's four main islands, **Kyushu** has always set itself apart from the others. Its climate is distinctly Mediterranean and even subtropical at its southern tip, and its inhabitants are known for being friendlier, more open, and even more "Westernized" than their compatriots in the rest of the country. Kyushu is also the most volcanic of Japan's islands, famous for its flourishing hot-spring resorts and several active volcanoes. It is a terrific place to explore if you have the time. If you can afford the "bullet train" just once, this is your chance, as—in one exhilarating sweep—you pass through almost all the major cities of Central and Western Honshu on the way.

Easily accessible from the Asian mainland via Korea, Kyushu has a longer history of significant contacts with foreigners than any other part of Japan. This was especially the case after it found itself on the southern route taken by European merchants and missionaries of the 16th century. Indeed, the famous port city of Nagasaki served as Japan's sole point of contact with the outside world during 260 years of self-imposed isolation.

Kyushu enjoys its special place in the national mythology as the cradle of Japanese civilization, despite the support of only a meager amount of archeological evidence. Legend tells of the Sun Goddess Amaterasu sending her grandson to Mt. Takachiho in central Kyushu, armed with the imperial mirror, sword, and jewel that Jimmu (Japan's first emperor) used on his conquest of the Yamato Plain near Nara. Modern historians' version is rather less exotic: Jimmu was probably a pirate from Okinawa who settled in Kyushu before launching his campaign to conquer Honshu.

The island's next important historical encounter was with the Mongols under Kublai Khan, when Kyushu was the target of abortive assaults in 1274 and 1281. The islanders' heroic resistance, admittedly abetted by a timely typhoon *(kamikaze:* "divine wind"), earned them a formidable martial reputation. The island proved to be the last bastion of the samurai ideal, when disenfranchised warriors launched the doomed Satsuma Rebellion in their desperation to forestall the relentless march of progress. It was in Kagoshima that the Imperial Japanese Navy was created from the nucleus of ships bought from the British at the end of the 19th century.

Portuguese merchants arrived in Kagoshima in 1543, with the missionaries of St. Francis Xavier following close behind. In addition to becoming a center of Western trade, Nagasaki provided a firm foothold in Japan for the Catholic Church—today much revived after 250 years of brutal suppression under the Tokugawa shoguns.

Northern Kyushu

Fukuoka is Kyushu's main commercial center, where you can tour the lively shopping district around the main station at Hakata. The delicate Hakataningyo dolls (the town's specialty craft) make attractive gifts, although as works of art for adults rather than toys for children. Bayside Place is a thriving nighttime eating and entertainment district built alongside Hakata wharf in the old merchant district, with attractively illuminated sculptures adding to the atmosphere. Enthusiastic and adventurous eaters should also look out for the numerous food stalls *(yatai)* found throughout the city, especially those offering Hakata *ramen* noodles, famed throughout Japan. Otherwise, Fukuoka mainly serves as the launching point for your exploration of the bulk of Kyushu to the south.

The first stop on the east coast is **Beppu**—perhaps the busiest and certainly the most intense spa town in Japan, with a permanent population of just 150,000 but about 13 million visitors a year. The Beppu district boasts eight different hot-spring areas, each with different properties. These include a hot waterfall at the Shibaseki spring, hot sand at Takegawara, hot mud at Kannawa, and picturesque outdoor baths in hot ponds among the rocks of the aptly named Hotta Hot Springs.

Kyushu

Iki Is.
Izuhara

Higashi-Fukawa
Kogushi
Hagi
Yamaguchi
Hofu

Katsumoto
Shimonoseki
Kita-kyushu
Ube
Tokuyama

Genkai
Sea
Nogata
Yukuhashi
Suo Sea

Gonoura
Iki Channel
Hizaki
Nakatsu

Karatsu
Fukae
Fukuoka
Ono
Tagawa
Takada
Kunisaki
Pen.

N

Amagi

Sasebo
Saga
Tosu
Beppu
Beppu Bay
Saganoseki

Ureshino
Kurume
Oita
Tsurusaki

Kashima
Aso
Taketa
Usuki

Bungu
Omura
Bay
Omura
Ariake
Sea
Omuta
National
Park
Saiki

Nagasaki
Shimabara
Kumamoto
Tsurumi-zaki

Shimabara Sea
Shimabara
Pen.
Matsubase

Nomo
Amakusa Sea
Unzen-
Amakusa
National
Marukchibi

Hondo
Yatsushiro

Amakusa Islands
Yatsushiro Bay
Yatsushiro

Nobeoka

Minamata
Hitoyoshi

Tsuno

Akune
Okuchi
Naka-Harada
Takanabe

Kami-Koshiki Is.
Sendai
Kabayashi
Sadowara
Miyazaki

Kamo
Kajiki
Jogasaki

Koshiki Strait
Kushikino
Kokubu
Miyakonojo

Shimo-
Koshiki Is.
Kagoshima
Sueyoshi
Shibushi

Cape Noma
Taniyama

PACIFIC
OCEAN

Kagoshima
Bay
Kanoya
Shibushi Bay

Makurazuki
O-Nejime
Cape Toi

Yamagawa

Cape Sata

Osumi Straits

Nishinoomote
0   100 mi.

0   100 km

Tanega
Anjo

159

Beppu's most popular attractions are the open-air "hell ponds" around Kannawa, which are alternately hilarious and dramatic. In the open-air Umi Jigoku ("Ocean Hell") you can buy eggs hard-boiled in a basket. In Oniyama Jigoku ("Devil's Mountain Hell"), a hundred crocodiles enjoy a hot soak. Chinoike Jigoku ("Blood Pool Hell") is a

---

Kyushu Museums

Fukuoka Art Museum located in Ohori Park, 1-6 Ohori-koen, Chuo-ku, Fukuoka; Tel. (0927) 146051. Open 9:30am–5pm daily except Mondays. Admission ¥200.

Nagasaki Municipal Museum Heiwa Kaikan, 7-8 Hirano-machi, Nagasaki; Tel. (0958) 458188. Open 9am–5pm daily except Mondays. Admission ¥100.

Nagasaki Atomic Bomb Museum take trams #1 or #3 from JR Nagasaki Station bound for Akasako, exit at Hamaguchi-machi stop; Tel. (0958) 441231. Open 8:30am–5:30pm daily. Admission ¥200 (adults), ¥100 (children).

Yufuin Folk Craft Museum 20-minute walk from Yufuin Station; Tel. (0977) 845850. Open daily 9am–5pm. Free admission.

Aso Volcanic Museum take bus to mountain top from JR Aso Station; Tel. (0967) 342111. Open daily 9am–5pm. Admission ¥840 (adults), ¥420 (children).

Miyazaki Prefectural Museum 2-4-4 Jingu, Miyazaki; Tel. (0985) 242071. Open 9am–4:30pm daily except Mondays. Admission ¥300 (adults), ¥200 (students), ¥100 (children).

Kagoshima Takamori Saigo Museum 7-minute walk from Nishi-Kagoshima Station, or 2-minute tram ride to Takamibashi stop; Tel. (0992) 397700. Open daily 9am–5pm. Admission ¥300 (adults), ¥150 (children).

Kagoshima Shoko Shuseikan Museum 6 minutes by bus from JR Kagoshima Station; Tel. (0992) 471511. Open daily 8:30am–5:30pm. Admission ¥300 (adults), ¥100 (children).

Beppu's "hell ponds" are an enduring fascination; it's easy to see why the sulfurous fumes are called the "Breath of the Earth."

steaming pond turned blood-red by its iron oxide. At the northern edge of the district is Bozu Jigoku ("Monk's Hell"), an obscenely bubbling mud pond where a Buddhist temple once stood until it was submerged in an earthquake back in the 15th century.

Also near Kannawa are several hot-spring developments, including attractive open-air rock pools and mineral mud baths with a "You've got it? We'll cure it!" reputation. But if heat is your thing, pay a visit to the grand old Meiji-era Takegawara public baths, not far from the JR train station. The old wooden building is simply magnificent, although its hot bath is one of the most basic you're likely to encounter. For just ¥620 you can lie down and have hot sand raked over you by a grinning, grandmotherly attendant—a ten-minute ordeal you'll never forget.

A gentle landscape of paddy fields reveals the serene side of Kyushu.

One unusual attraction not mentioned in the official tourist literature is Beppu's "sex museum," which is famous throughout Japan. There are several such collections in Japan, consisting of bizarre images, sculptures, and elaborate dioramas depicting many of the darker aspects of human sexuality, often with fantasies involving demons and monsters perpetrating unspeakable deeds upon helpless mortals. This is another "only in Japan" experience, one definitely not for the faint-hearted.

The rural village of **Yufuin** is relaxed, gentle, and charming, featuring old-fashioned farmhouses around tiny Kinrinko Lake. Set at the foot of Mt. Yufu—an extinct volcano covered by dense bamboo forest—Yufuin is famous for its hot-spring baths, most of which you can try for just a few hundred yen. The helpful tourist information desk in the JR station can direct you to the most popular or unusual spots, especially those with outdoor baths *(rotenburo)*.

162

The excellent Folk Craft Museum in an old manor house holds regular demonstrations of local arts and crafts. Hard-core seekers of local culture will find a single day insufficient for visiting Yufuin's Museum of Modern Art, the unexpected **Marc Chagall Museum**, and 15 other art galleries. The gentle paths along the small rivers that meander through the town provide serene views of ricefields and superb scenery.

Farther south, the thick groves of palm trees lining the coast at **Miyazaki** serve as a reminder of its position on the edge of the tropics. This resort town has a long and usually uncrowded sandy beach, and there are several pleasant golf courses among the palm trees.

Heiwadai Park brings together the prehistoric past and the frequently strange present. The park's prefectural museum displays some small clay figures *(haniwa)* unearthed at nearby ancient burial mounds, together with pots, tools, and weapons dating back to as early as 10,000 B.C. The grounds are dominated by the bizarre and grandiose Peace Tower, which, curiously, was erected in 1940. At that time it had a different name: Hakko-ichi-wu ("Eight World Regions Under One Roof"), embodying the militarist aims of the Imperial Japanese Army. More palatable in its goal is the park's Miyazaki Shrine, dedicated to Japan's quasi-legendary first emperor, Jimmu, who reputedly commenced his glorious career in this region.

Just north of Miyazaki is one of the many results of Japan's grandiose spending projects that characterized the "bubble economy" years of the 1980s and early 1990s. **Seagaia Ocean Dome**, the largest indoor water park in the world, comprises an artificially landscaped beach complete with palm trees and a giant wave pool to complete the illusion of a tropical paradise. The facilities are enclosed within a huge retractable roof.

South of Miyazaki, the little island of **Aoshima** is connected to Kyushu by a footbridge and surrounded by strange, wave-like rocks believed to be between 15 million and 30 million years old. Beyond Aoshima the picturesque, winding Nichinan coast alternates rugged cliffs with some fine sandy bathing beaches. The seafood along this coast is especially good: try the reasonably priced lobster and giant periwinkles.

Southern Kyushu

Kagoshima dominates the head of a deep indentation at the southern tip of Kyushu, and its harbor has played a prominent role in Japanese military history. It was here that the Portuguese landed, bringing to Japan for the first time bread, guns, and Christianity. The sailors' first landfall was on the little offshore island of Tanegashima, which has progressed from matchlocks and muskets to being Japan's principal rocket-launching center.

It was from Kagoshima that the last desperate sorties of World War II were begun to resist an imminent US invasion, including the *kamikaze* raids on American warships. Inevitably, devastating bombing reprisals flattened the city. But modern Kagoshima is now an attractive green and airy place, with wide boulevards, delightful parks, and a couple of intriguing historical museums.

Shiroyama Park (southwest of Kagoshima Station) is up on a hill, giving you a fine view of the city and Kagoshima Bay through the archway of Nanshu Shrine. This shrine is dedicated to Kyushu's most celebrated son and one of Japan's national heroes, Takamori Saigo, last great champion of the samurai. He is buried with 2,023 of his warriors, who died in the ill-fated 1877 Satsuma Rebellion. This was the last stand of the samurai against the overthrow of their time-honored privileges. Many of the soldiers, like Takamori himself, died by their own hand in a final gesture of defiance. A museum in the park is devoted to his life and battles. Nearby, the history of the Kagoshima region is nicely summed up in the ultramodern **Reimeikan Prefectural Museum**, which includes local arts and crafts as well as examples of those first Portuguese matchlock rifles.

A couple of miles or so north of Kagoshima Station are the lovely **Iso Gardens**, also landscaped on a hill, where the lord of Satsuma had his villa. Be sure to visit the **Shoko Shuseikan Museum**, housed in an old factory established here by the forward-looking leader for arms manufacture and other new industries.

Out in the bay—towering over the entire peninsula—is Japan's most notoriously active volcano, the huge three-coned **Sakurajima**,

The Okinawa Islands

Returned to Japanese sovereignty in 1972, after 27 years of postwar US occupation, Japan's own tropical paradise can be reached by plane (1 hour 35 minutes) from Fukuoka on Kyushu. The main attraction in this string of islands is island-hopping in search of perfect beaches and coral reefs, with some of the best swimming at Nakadomari's Moon Beach. Okinawa comprises 57 islands altogether, 40 of which are inhabited.

The main city on Okinawa's main island is Naha, which is overwhelming influenced by the postwar American military presence. The island's military bases are still home to tens of thousands of US servicemen and dependents. The vast selection of army surplus junk (such as bullet and shell casings) on sale in central Naha is certainly a strange one. Not surprisingly, there is a boisterous nightlife and busy red-light district—Naha was the friendly setting of the Marlon Brando film Teahouse of the August Moon.

Among Okinawa's many special attractions are the rural bullfights in the villages north of Naha. These contests pitch bull against bull on the same principle as sumo wrestling, as one entrant attempts to push the other out of the ring, not to kill him. The local taste in entertainment also runs to more grisly events: the public fights to the death between mongoose and cobra, staged by gamblers for high stakes.

Undeniably spectacular is Gyokusendo Cave, situated 12 km (7.5 miles) southwest of Naha, near the village of Minatogawa. Extending over a mile, it is adorned by a half-million stalactites and stalagmites among crystal-clear streams and hordes of friendly little bats.

which sends up tremendous black and white clouds of ash and steam. Take a taxi or bus (from Kagoshima Station) for a closer look at the lava and a fine view of the whole Kagoshima Bay area. The Sakurajima peninsula was once an island until a gigantic eruption in 1914, when the rocks and lava joined it forever to the mainland. A powerful illustration of the magnitude of the eruption is found at Haragosha Shrine, where you can just see the top cross bar of the shrine's arch, the rest submerged by hardened lava.

St. Francis Xavier Memorial Church, in Xavier Park (tram to Takamibaba stop), was built in 1949 to commemorate the 400th anniversary of the arrival of the Jesuit missionary. His statue—inexplicably pinned halfway up a monolith in a very martyr-like pose, although he died in his bed (in China)—stands with its back to the sea beside a sculpted frieze dedicated to the suffering of his Japanese converts.

Ibusuki, south of Kagoshima, is a hot-spring resort that caters to honeymoon couples—hundreds of them at a time. However, the main draw is its famous natural sand bath. Clad only in a cotton kimono, you lie down for attendants to bury you up to the neck in sand at a medium-broil temperature. Just stare up at the sky while you sweat off a few pounds and the attendant shovels on fresh sand. As the local chamber of commerce hilariously puts it: "It is not only effective for overall beauty, but also for whiplash injuries caused by traffic accidents, and popular with newlyweds." A more cynical view is that the sands provide a cure for which there is no known disease.

Chiran (80 minutes inland by bus from Kagoshima) is a peaceful, secluded 18th-century samurai village. In classically narrow, zigzagging lanes designed to hinder surprise attack, the houses, today still inhabited by the Satsuma warriors' descendants, offer the rare opportunity to visit some exquisite private gardens, otherwise carefully concealed behind tall hedges. The simple, serene style of landscaping, with rocks, gravel, and a few shrubs, draws on the precepts of Zen Buddhism that had such a special appeal for the austere samurai.

Chiran's **Kamikaze Museum**, which includes a monumental statue of a pilot, exhibits the young men's uniforms, helmets, and final letters to their families explaining that they were continuing the samurai spirit of defending the country's traditional values. There are also full-scale models of the planes, with a fuel tank big enough for only a one-way mission.

Western Kyushu

Halfway back along Kyushu's west coast, Kumamoto is an old castle town that was of considerable importance to the Tokugawa shoguns as a counterweight to the presence of the annoyingly independent Shimazu clan down in Kagoshima. For visitors today, Kumamoto serves as a convenient gateway for the scenic road trip to the Mt. Aso volcano or a ferry cruise to the Unzen-Amakusa National Park.

Buried alive: hot volcanic sand therapy at Surigahama Beach, Ibusuki.

Festival decorations brighten up the scene at Unzen, a popular resort spa area in western Kyushu.

The reconstructed **Kumamoto Castle** is worth a visit for the significant role it played during the last hectic days of Japan's feudal era. Once a vast fortification of 49 turrets, it ranked alongside Osaka and Nagoya as one of the country's greatest impregnable bastions. The 1960 ferroconcrete reconstruction of the main castle-keep houses a fine museum of feudal armor and weapons and offers a good view of the city.

Suizenji Park is an extravagant but attractive example of the extensive gardens of the 17th century. Here, designers have reproduced a miniature version of all the major landscape features along the old Tokaido Highway between Kyoto and Edo—including, of course, a small artificial version of Mt. Fuji.

The bus ride from Kumamoto to the mighty **Mt. Aso** volcano takes you across some gently rolling hills, past orange groves, fields of watermelon, and the special grass used for *tatami* mats. There is even a rare sight of yellow wheat fields—grown for beer and noodles rather than for bread (which is mostly imported). The panorama of the five volcanic craters of Mt. Aso blends vivid emerald-green mounds with great carpets of pink azaleas on the surrounding slopes and plateau. Only one of the craters, Nakadake, is still really active. But it is well worth a visit to the top (a short hike from the bus stop) to peer down into the bleak, barren crater emitting puffs of sulfurous fumes and contrasting starkly with the colorful vegetation all around it.

On your way back down, allow enough time to visit the fascinating **Aso Volcanic Museum**. This has some very realistic audio-visual re-enactments of eruptions and earthquakes, with special stereo sound effects. Three-dimensional models of exploding mountains and molten lava flows from all over the world are shown. You can press a button to see America's Mt. St Helen's blow its top, or you can relive the astonishing 1933 eruption of Mt. Aso itself.

The **Unzen-Amakusa National Park**, consisting of a peninsula and islands west of Kumamoto, is most pleasantly reached on a picturesque one-hour ferry trip from the nearby port of Misumi to Shimabara. The harbor is dotted with the pine-covered islands of Tsukumo, offering delightful bathing along white-sand beaches. Unzen itself, once the favored "hill station" of Europeans escaping the steaming summers of the Asian mainland, is now a rather noisy, crowded spa resort. It serves best as an overnight stay prior to an early morning hike around the Unzen volcano's craters. The volcano last erupted in spring 1991, but it is no longer considered dangerous.

Nagasaki

Nagasaki is an unexpectedly charming city. To a large extent, this reflects its unbroken experience of more than four centuries of hospitality to foreigners—Chinese, Portuguese, and Dutch—during a period in Japanese history when the country was characterized by often murderous xenophobia. It is also a surprisingly attractive town:

sadly, a relative rarity among Japan's bland, homogenous cities. Its natural harbor, surrounded by green hills, is one of the most attractive in the world. Indeed, the city's distinct geography allowed most of its older neighborhoods to survive the terrible destruction wrought by the second atomic bomb to be dropped on Japan, on 9 August 1945 —despite the fact that the Nagasaki bomb was more powerful than the one dropped on Hiroshima three days earlier.

Long before the arrival of the first Europeans, Nagasaki had been a major focus of Japan's trade with China. Indeed, the Chinese influence in the city is clearly noticeable even today. Major Buddhist temples, profiting from the suppression of Christianity during the 17th century, were established by Chinese Zen monks and designed in the style of the late Ming Dynasty. On a more mundane contemporary level, the most popular Nagasaki lunch is a solid, nourishing bowl of *chanpon:* Chinese noodles in a tangy fish broth laden with a cornucopia of mushrooms, fish, prawns, vegetables, and other goodies.

Near the centrally located Japan Railways station is the first sign of the Portuguese role in the city's fascinating history. A monument to 26 Christian martyrs executed in 1597 (at the beginning of Japan's repression of Catholicism) includes a small museum displaying relics, including a communion wafer that has survived in dehydrated form since the 17th century. The museum describes how other Christians were boiled alive in 1615 at the nearby Unzen hot springs. (Bear in mind, of course, that equally cruel religious persecution of Catholics, Protestants, and Jews was quite common in Europe at that time.)

Even after the persecution and banishing of missionaries and the ban on Christianity, Nagasaki's Catholics still managed—at great risk—to continue clandestine observance throughout the years of the Tokugawa shogunate. They even went to Buddhist temples to worship the feminine Kannon deities, which were resculpted holding a child to represent Mary and Jesus.

The Dutch, however, being nonproselytizing Protestants, were allowed to stay on throughout Japan's centuries of isolation. Their little community on Dejima Island, in Nagasaki Bay, sheltered the only remaining foreigners left in the country. *Oranda-san* ("Dutch people") eventually became the accepted term for all foreigners in Japan.

To get a good sense of Nagasaki's personality, start down at the harbor. Boat tours begin from the pier at Ohata Port Terminal, taking you on a fascinating 50-minute cruise around Nagasaki Bay. Your excursion steamer will feel like a child's toy as it passes the gigantic supertankers of the Mitsubishi Shipyard. Now the largest private shipyard in the world, this was the intended target that the US Air Force B-52 missed when it dropped the second atomic bomb.

Dejima Pier has been reconnected to the mainland from what was once the Dutch island concession. The museum here has interesting relics of the Dutch community. In front of the museum is a model of the neat little settlement they established in 1609, when the only Japanese permitted to visit were trading partners and prostitutes. Commerce has always been an effective bridge of cultural barriers.

To see how the Dutch of a later era lived, climb the cobbled street of **Hollander Slope** (number 5 tram to the Ishibashi stop), where you'll see some red-brick and wooden clapboard houses with colonial-style verandahs and—a rare sight atop houses in Japan—chimneys. The houses are an enduring monument to the privileged position of the foreigners allowed to live here.

The British presence in 19th-century Nagasaki is nostalgically commemorated at the hillside **Glover Gardens**, a short distance west of Hollander Slope. Escalators take you up to the houses of British traders. To the delighted curiosity of Japanese visitors, the houses are filled with the kind of Victorian paraphernalia that is becoming increasingly popular in modern Japan: damask-covered furniture, an upright piano, a massive mahogany sideboard, and a grand old gramophone with a big horn, manufactured by the Nippon-Ophone Company.

Kofukuji temple was the first of the Zen Buddhist temples built by the Chinese (1620) after the Tokugawa shoguns had outlawed Christianity and ordered citizens to register as Buddhists. In a pic-

Interior of the Sofukuji temple, a striking example of late Ming Dynasty architecture.

turesque setting with palm trees in the courtyard, the temple's architecture and sculpture are typical of southern China. Kofukuji also offers (by advanced reservation) a frugal but tasty vegetarian meal cooked by the priests themselves. Meal times are announced by the beating of a big red "fish" gong.

The pride and joy of the neighborhood is the **Meganebashi**, a double-arched stone bridge across the Nakajima River. It was built in 1634 by the abbot of Kofukuji and is the oldest of its kind in the country. The reflection of the double arches in the river on a fairly calm day creates a visual image resembling a pair of eyeglasses. The narrow streets bordering the river are full of interesting antique stores, coffee shops, and restaurants.

Sofukuji temple (1629) is a handsome example of late Ming Dynasty architecture, with its striking vermilion-painted, stone-arched tower gate. In the courtyard is a huge iron cauldron that was used for distributing rice gruel to the poor during famines in the 17th and 19th centuries. The Chinese Buddha statues here are notable for their variously proud, cheerful, or humble stances not to be seen in the Buddhas of Japanese temples.

The **Nagasaki Peace Park** embraces the epicenter of the atomic blast that left 73,884 people dead, 74,904 injured, and a miraculous

71,585 unscathed. The hills surrounding the city did much to contain the subsequent atomic fallout. The park features a monumental sculpture (by local artist Kitamura Seibo) that stirred considerable controversy when unveiled in 1955. The massive figure's right hand points skyward—toward the actual point of detonation—as a warning of the constant threat of nuclear weapons, while his left hand stretches out in a gesture of universal peace. As in Hiroshima, one of the most moving monuments is a single piece of masonry left standing. In this case, it is the red-brick and gray-stone remains of an arch from the Urakami Catholic Church, at the time the largest church in Asia.

A visit to Nagasaki is meaningless without a stop at its provocative and challenging **Atomic Bomb Museum**. The exhibits power fully document the build-up to the dropping of the atomic bomb on Nagasaki and the appalling effects of the blast itself and its aftermath. The curators have done a good job of separating any military justification for the decision from its tragic consequences for the civilian population. Like the Hiroshima museum, the final message is not of victims demanding sympathy but of an entire community committed to total nuclear disarmament for the sake of the entire planet, with its own message of "Never again."

Finally, at the end of a long day, take the cable car to the top of **Mt. Inasa**, 332 m (1,089 ft) high, for a dramatic sunset view of Nagasaki and its harbor as city lights begin to sparkle.

NORTHERN HONSHU AND HOKKAIDO

The regions of Japan to the northeast of Tokyo are more sparsely inhabited and tend to be less often visited by tourists, either foreign or Japanese. But both northern Honshu—which is more commonly known as "Tohoku"—and the northernmost island of Hokkaido offer the advantage of unspoiled countryside and friendly down-to-earth villagers still imbued with something of a frontier spirit. Their folkcrafts are authentic and much less commercialized than in most other parts of Japan. And their festivals, in an area without the usual

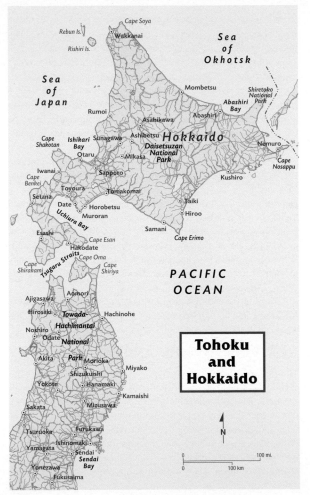

Cape Soya
Wakkanai
Rebun Is.
Rishiri Is.

Sea
of
Okhotsk

Mombetsu
Shiretoko
National
Park
Abashiri
Bay
Abashiri

Sea
of
Japan

Rumoi
Asahikawa
Hokkaido

Cape
Shakotan
Ishikari
Bay
Sunagawa
Ashibetsu
Daisetsuzan
National
Park
Nemuro
Cape
Nosappu

Otaru
Mikasa

Iwanai
Sapporo
Kushiro

Cape
Benkei
Toyoura

Setana
Date
Tomakomai

Horobetsu
Muroran
Taiki
Hiroo

Uchiura Bay
Samani
Cape Erimo

Esashi
Cape Esan

Hakodate
PACIFIC
OCEAN

Cape
Shirakami
Cape Oma
Cape
Shiriya

Ajigasawa
Aomori

Hirosaki
Hachinohe

Noshiro
Towada-
Hachimantai

Odate
National

Akita
Park
Morioka

Shizukuishi
Miyako

Yokote
Hanamaki

Mizusawa
Kamaishi

Sakata

Tsuruoka
Furukawa

Yamagata
Ishinomaki
Sendai
Yonezawa
Sendai
Bay
Fukusaima

Tohoku
and
Hokkaido

N

0   100 mi.
0   100 km

174

sorts of urban entertainment, are frequent, colorful, and more spontaneous than in the more densely populated regions of the country. No overall picture of Japanese life can be complete without a short visit to these northern territories.

Tohoku

Until the Tokugawa shoguns completed their conquest of all Japan from the 17th century on, the towns of **Tohoku** constituted the northern boundaries of the Japanese empire. Beyond them were the tribes of the native Ainu, at that time not considered "Japanese." It was only when the Ainu were progressively driven north up into Hokkaido that Tohoku was opened up to broader settlement.

Its massive rice yield (as much as 20 percent of the national rice crop) has made Tohoku the chief supplier of the country's needs. Thus, the general trend for more and more peasants to drift away from the land to the cities has been noticeably less marked here. The very remoteness of Tohoku was appealing to such religious groups as the Zen Buddhists, who espouse an ascetic, unworldly life and constructed some of the country's finest Buddhist temples in this northern part of Honshu.

Matsushima is considered one of the country's three Great Scenic Beauties (part of the Japanese passion for cataloging things in three of this or eight of that.) Although you can reach Matsushima in 40 minutes by train from Sendai, the best way is to stop off at Shiogama and take the one-hour boat cruise across Matsushima Bay. Scores of tiny islands dot the bay, their white sandstone shaped by the elements into arches, caves, and pyramids and covered with lovely, wispy sea pines. The changing perspective as you cruise slowly past is extraordinary.

In the town of Matsushima, visit the pretty Kanrantei Pavilion for one of the best views of the bay from a rocky cliff beside the landing stage for the cruise ships. But practically any point on the hills rising behind the town will offer you a spectacular view.

Zuiganji temple is the center of an old Zen Buddhist seminary. The buildings were constructed in 1609 by the lord of Tohoku, Masamune Date. In the temple's treasure house you can see a statue of the crusty old warlord in all his armor. He lost his right eye—from smallpox, not in battle—and was nicknamed Dokugan-ryu ("One-Eyed Dragon"). As you walk up the long cedar-shaded avenue to the temple, notice the two-story caves hewn from the rock that serve as accommodation for itinerant monks.

In the town of Hiraizumi—just a 20-minutes bus ride from Ichi-no-seki Station—you'll find a temple dating from the late Heian period (early 12th century). **Chusonji** was erected by the Fujiwara family when their power behind the imperial throne in Kyoto was waning. Two of the temple's structures have survived the countless wars of the Fujiwara. The Konjikido (Golden Hall) is a fabulously opulent mausoleum that Kiyohira Fujiwara built for himself in 1124. Everything except the uppermost roof covering is coated in pure gold. This priceless treasure, now protected by glass inside a fireproof concrete Kamakura-style hall, is believed to be what Columbus was after in his search for the country he called Chipangu. The Kyozo is even older (1108) and used to house the temple's Buddhist scriptures *(sutras)*, which are now kept in the modern treasure house.

Hokkaido

Not opened up to full-scale settlement until after the Meiji Restoration of 1868, the island of **Hokkaido** is Japan's "Far North." Here are some of the few Japanese who enjoy uncrowded cities, unspoiled wilderness, and a simpler existence in a climate and landscape comparable to Scandinavia: snowcapped mountains and pine forest, with a subarctic climate in the northernmost area. The island's capital, **Sapporo**, was a natural choice for Japan's first Winter Olympic

Unspoiled beauty: Matsushima Bay, with its scores of tiny islands and sandstone rocks sculpted by the elements.

Games in 1972. Yet in the summer months Hokkaido's mountains and lake country are mild enough for good camping and hiking.

At the end of the 19th century unemployed samurai—adventurous but still attached to the old traditions—took their families to Hokkaido to carve out a new life for themselves. American advisers helped to develop Hokkaido's agriculture and coal mining industries and to lay out an urban grid system for Sapporo.

After years of neglect and discrimination, the cultural significance of the tiny though historically significant Ainu community is finally being recognized. Hokkaido now has some fascinating museums devoted to Ainu life, and the village of Shiraoi preserves the artifacts and folkcrafts of their culture.

Sapporo

One of the most attractive postwar urban innovations in Japan is Sapporo's **Odori Promenade**, a broad green boulevard lined with flower beds, lilacs, and maples—and with fountains down the middle, running east to west for a straight mile. It's a great place to start your visit.

Sapporo has a nationwide reputation for its beer, introduced in the 1870s by a German brewer who recognized the surrounding country's hop-growing potential. The beer garden, to the northeast of the downtown area, is a lusty place to sample the town's frontier spirit.

Around the Island

Lake Shikotsu, a volcanic crater lake situated 26 km (16 miles) west of Chitose airport, provides one of southern Hokkaido's most picturesque camping and hiking areas. There's great salmon fishing here each year starting in May.

Not far from the spa town of Noboribetsu is **Shiraoi**, a well-reconstructed Ainu village complete with artisans demonstrating traditional arts and crafts. The superb **Ainu Museum**, established with the help of European and American anthropologists, features a vivid exhibition of Ainu history.

WHAT TO DO

SHOPPING

Modern Japan has embraced the consumer society to such an extent that shopping can be a full-time pursuit. The Japanese themselves (in the big cities at least) can be seen more often than not with some kind of shopping bag—they make very large, sturdy ones—just on the off chance that they might want to buy something. You cannot get to know this country properly, even if you don't want to buy anything, without exploring the rich and varied range of traditional arts and crafts, the famous cornucopia of electronic gadgets and precision instruments, or the impressively awful selection of kitsch souvenirs in the major tourist centers.

Japan is notoriously expensive, so don't expect fabulous bargains. The country has succeeded economically by fixing the best price it can get for everything, but the domestic market pays high prices because of a stiff sales tax and surprisingly convoluted and inefficient distribution systems. Japanese tourists visiting other countries are still shocked to find Japanese consumer goods available for far less than they have to pay at home.

> Can't decide which way to dodge people coming your way on a crowded sidewalk? The Japanese usually pass on the left.

Start by looking at the range of goods in the department stores and hundreds of specialty shops in the underground shopping centers before going off to find better prices at discount shops. Department stores generally offer superb selections of everything—but at Japan's highest prices.

You might be tempted to do your shopping at the end of your trip so you won't have to drag all that electronic equipment, lacquerware, ceramics, or whatever around the country with you. Instead, consider buying everything you want as you go along, using Japan's remarkably efficient and inexpensive *takkyubin* courier delivery services (available at the ubiquitous convenience stores) to forward your larger purchases to your hotel, where they will be waiting for you on your return to Tokyo or elsewhere. Given Japan's relatively low crime rates, you can be sure you'll be reunited with your precious souvenirs.

Hi-Tech Products

In Tokyo, the place to go for every electronic and computer item imaginable—and plenty that you didn't even know existed—is Akihabara, an entire district devoted to specialty stores selling mountains of electronic equipment often at very low prices. The

larger stores usually have a tax-free department offering a narrower range of products designed for use abroad. English-speaking sales staff are often on hand, but don't expect the same discount prices that are offered on the other floors, despite the tax-free incentive.

One draw for visiting gadget freaks is being able to buy the very latest equipment several months ahead of its sales launch abroad. However, cameras and electronic goods are rarely available at better prices than those in New York City, still the world's reigning discount center. Those hunting for computer software and hardware should not expect to find anything other than Japanese-language products for sale.

Osaka's equivalent hi-tech shopping district is Nipponbashi, a very

poor relation to Akihabara with neither the range nor the prices available in Tokyo.

Note that local electric current is 100 volts/50 (or 60) cycles, which is slightly different from the US and completely different from Europe. Therefore, if you don't want to bother with converters, stick to the top-floor tax-free department specializing in export goods designed for use around the world. Also note that Japanese VCRs and TVs are designed for NTSC, the same broadcast system used in North America. If you plan to buy

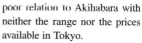

Inside Akihabara you'll find every electronic gizmo and doodad you ever imagined.

anything for use in Europe or elsewhere (where PAL is the main broadcast standard), make sure you purchase a multisystem unit; only these are compatible with the various broadcast standards in use around the globe.

Cameras. As an exception to the general rule of not making big purchases until near the end of your visit, it makes sense to buy camera equipment as soon as possible so you can try it out during the trip. If a fault occurs, you can arrange to have it repaired or exchanged before you leave. Most stores are good about exchanging faulty goods. Note, though, that warranties are often valid in Japan only, so check with the manufacturer for details of upgrading to worldwide coverage. Shinjuku has Tokyo's largest discount camera stores, although these rarely offer better prices than those available from New York's famous mail-order outlets.

> **Don't be surprised to see adults reading comic books on the train. Pop culture reading sells by the millions here.**

Traditional Goods

Kimono. Japanese silk kimono are magnificent but staggeringly expensive. Most Japanese people save up for years to buy one and then often spend an equal amount of time in debt after making the investment. If you're not among the world's wealthiest tourists, the good news is that new and nearly new kimono are usually sold for a tiny fraction of their new prices at the big flea markets held at temples, shrines, and other large communal sites. Many Japanese are highly superstitious about acquiring second-hand goods, especially clothing. In Tokyo, try the weekend market at Harajuku, and check the English-language press for details of shrine and temple markets. Kyoto's two biggest flea markets are held at Toji temple (the 21st of each month) and at Kitano Temmangu shrine (25th), but there are many others.

Another alternative is the more modest but still elegant *yukata* (light cotton kimono), traditionally in indigo-blue and white and

Japanese silk kimono are veritable works of art—and this is reflected in the staggering prices.

much, much cheaper than anything made of silk. Also look out for the silk *obi* sashes used to tie kimono. Some are magnificently decorative in their own right; if you don't want to wear one, consider an obi as an original and unusual wall-hanging in a Western home.

Antiques. For antique furniture and miscellaneous items, Kyoto's famous geisha district of Gion has one of the finest selections in Japan. Even if you're just browsing, the shops on Nawate-dori, Furomonzen-dori, and Shinmonzen-dori offer a superb selection of antique furniture, ceramics, masks, lacquerware, and Buddhist objects.

Artwork. Attractively colorful *ukiyo-e* woodblock prints and scroll paintings can be found in antique stores, second-hand bookstores, and even temple markets. Prices vary enormously, so shopping around usually pays off handsomely.

Pottery and ceramics. These are very much a living tradition that has maintained its high standards. Most regions have their own distinct styles, varying from Kyoto's ornate and highly glazed *kiyomizu-yaki* to the beautiful natural earthenware of Bizen in Okayama and of Shigaraki near Kyoto. The town of Mashiko, to the north of Tokyo, is well worth a day's train excursion if you are interested in seeing how some of Japan's most celebrated pottery is made; the prices here are slightly better than back in Tokyo. You can also stay for lessons.

Knick-knack addict? A browse through this store in Doguya-suji, Osaka, reveals a wealth of traditional treasures to take home.

Lacquerware. You are least likely to go wrong in terms of uniformly high quality if you're in the market for lacquerware. Trays, plates, bowls, and jewelry boxes are superbly finished—and not so heavy as to create problems of excess baggage.

Paper goods. Fans, dolls, and hand-made stationery are usually reasonably priced but produced with the same meticulous care as are objects made from more precious materials.

Books. Tokyo's Kanda district is devoted almost entirely to second-hand books. The biggest neighborhood of its kind in the world, it sells books in most European languages as well as Japanese. You'll also find excellent old maps and prints here, but the merchants know the going price for everything; real bargains are few and far between.

ENTERTAINMENT

For information on all current Tokyo theater programs and show times, consult free weekly magazines such as *Tokyo Weekender* and *Tokyo Classified*, which are available in your hotel and in the foreign book sections of the Kinokuniya and Maruzen bookstores.

As one of the most vivid and important expressions of Japan's traditional cultural heritage, theater is an adventure in itself. Traditional Japanese drama, because of its stylization, extravagant gesture, and solemn or even bizarre intonation, might be difficult for Westerners. However, perseverance will be well rewarded once you get used to the conventions. The impact of the impassioned performances, aided by stunning costumes and elaborate make-up and masks, can be utterly seductive; many a skeptic has emerged an addict. Most Japanese theater aims less at developing a coherent plot, in the Western manner, than at creating a particular tone, atmosphere, and emotional extremes.

Noh

This is the oldest theatrical form, strictly speaking, and also the most austere and demanding. Derived originally from ritual dances

of the imperial court at Nara and Kyoto, in the 14th century *noh* became a fully developed masked drama of chanting, dancing, and highly stylized acting. A hero and just two or three supporting actors enact stories about gods, historic battles, ghosts, unhappy love, and grief-stricken insanity. The more somber themes alternate with *kyogen* farces about the life of the common people, which often feature a satirical element.

The commentary is chanted by a chorus of six to eight narrators (reminiscent of the chorus in Greek tragedy) who sit at the side of the stage, while musicians positioned at the back of the stage provide stark accompaniment with flute and drums. Contrasting with the resplendent costumes, the set has an austere simplicity: a backdrop (usually a permanent wall) of a large pine tree and some bamboo, with no curtain. The stage is framed by a classical Japanese tiled roof making a "house" inside the theater.

Male actors, in masks, play all the roles. Characters often take several minutes to enter and exit the stage, moving painfully slowly in one of Japan's greatest examples of form over function. For aficionados, a *noh* performance is an eclectic nirvana. For many others, it is powerfully soporific. Look around the audience and you'll see plenty of locals nodding off unselfconsciously.

Performances last several hours, with as many as five plays in a program. You can probably manage at least a couple, and theaters often provide a good buffet between plays. See the best ones at Tokyo's National Noh Theater, Kanze Kaikan at Shibuya, or Kyoto's National Noh Theater. Other fine troupes perform in Osaka and Kanazawa.

Kabuki

Ever since the Tokugawa shoguns restricted performances to the samurai classes, *noh* drama has had a rather elitist appeal. *Kabuki,*

Bugaku (traditional Shinto ritual dances) makes for a fascinating and unforgettable spectacle.

on the other hand, has proved much more popular. Equally stylized in its way, *kabuki* is filled with fantastic color, movement, action, drama, and comedy. The performers are folk heroes, and the greatest of them—descendants of centuries-old dynasties of actors—are declared "Living National Treasures." Audience participation is at fever pitch, with people yelling as their personal heroes enter: "We've waited for you!" or "You're the greatest in Japan!"

Nothing is spared in the way of costumes and décor; there is no such thing as "over the top." Ever since the 18th century, revolving stages and trapdoors have been employed for supernatural characters to rise to the stage. Popular, but art of the highest order, *kabuki* tells stories of horror, blood and thunder, and passionate love. Connoisseurs wait for the set pieces: the colorful parade of the courtesan, a poignant s*eppuku* suicide, the exciting fight scenes, and—summit of the art of *kabuki*—the end of a love affair that the heroine must break off, perhaps to save her lover's honor, but never because she no longer loves him.

> **People bring their lunch to the kabuki theater, stay all day, and shout out the names of their favorite actors when they appear on stage.**

"She" is in fact likely to be a 60-year-old man. In the early days of *kabuki,* at the beginning of the 17th century, the acclaimed Kyoto dancers started to present increasingly erotic and lascivious performances. With the audience's passionate loyalties to various star performers often leading to fights, the prudish Tokugawa shogunate decided to ban female performers, fearing a breakdown in all-important social order. However, they then found that the young men who took over the female roles were also attracting ardent devotees among military officers and even priests—homosexuality at that time was not yet frowned upon. So they were in turn replaced by older men. After years of study, these *onnagata* make an astoundingly subtle and delicate art of capturing the gestures and movements of both young girls and old crones.

Tokyo's Kabuki-za theater is the ideal venue for sampling a slice of Japan's ever-popular, age-old tradition of kabuki.

At Tokyo's Kabuki-za Theater, you can rent headphones for the performance, providing simultaneous English-language translation of the important dialogue along with explanations of the action and conventions. Shows last up to four hours, but you can buy cheaper balcony tickets for just part of the program. Kyoto's *kabuki* troupe performs in December and Osaka's in May.

Bunraku

Japan's celebrated puppet theater can be seen at the National Bunraku Theater in Osaka's Nipponbashi district, although performances are also put on several weeks each year at Tokyo's National Theater. Don't be misled: *bunraku* is theater for adults rather than children, using the

The entrance to Soemon-cho, one of central Osaka's premier nightlife and entertainment streets.

same dramatic themes, stories, and conventions as in *noh* and *kabuki* but achieving a unique impact with the almost life-sized, colorfully costumed puppets. The puppeteers, dressed all in black, are initially distractingly visible on stage, manipulating and walking around with their puppets—yet completely "disappear" from your perception as the magic of the drama sweeps you away. A detailed English explanation of the plot is always provided, and wireless recorded commentary units are sometimes available.

Bunraku's heyday was the beginning of the 18th century, when playwright Monzaemon Chikamatsu wrote works specifically for the puppets that are regarded as among the greatest achievements of Japanese literature. Heroism in battle and the noble values of the samurai tradition are the principal themes. It comes as quite a shock to watch a warrior performing his final gesture of ritual suicide and realize that it's only a puppet. The emotional effect is undiminished, and the gory effects are usually horribly creative.

Film

The Japanese cinema industry is in lingering recession, with growing numbers of people preferring to watch videos at home. Don't be surprised to see the latest Hollywood blockbusters on release. These attract bigger audiences than do current local offerings, which seem tawdry and unoriginal after the towering creativity of giants like Kurosawa and Oshima. Despite occasional surprise international successes (such as *Unagi* and *Shall We Dance?),* Japanese cinema will probably continue to be dominated by recycled ultraviolent gangster tales until it undergoes long-overdue industry reforms.

Nightlife

If you'd like to see how the Japanese handle Western-style popular music and dancing, you'll find good quality jazz clubs, conventional discos (with, naturally, fantastic electronic equipment), and even country-and-western saloons, all in Tokyo's cosmopolitan restaurant districts of Akasaka and Roppongi. Teenagers might like to join the open-air disco hordes at Harajuku, near Yoyogi Park.

FESTIVALS AND FOLKLORE

Despite increasing urbanization and social change, Japanese society retains its small, closely knit communities strongly dependent on

Shinto gods to ensure good harvests for survival. Forget the karaoke, the bullet trains, and all those mobile phones for a moment. With such a highly developed sense of ritual and tradition, Japan's *matsuri* (festivals) are much more than just fun for the community: for many they remain integral to life itself. There is at least one festival happening somewhere in Japan on any day of the year.

Each region has its own festivals or variations on the large national ones. Most honor either Shinto deities and shrines or major Buddhist temples. Buddhist festivals are usually fairly restrained affairs, often involving an important image of the Buddha that might be available for public viewing only on this occasion.

The real drama is at Shinto festivals. Some are austere purification ceremonies involving traditional music, chanting, dance, and often fire. At the opposite extreme are massive, almost riotous processions of thousands of bellowing, sweat-drenched men fighting to carry a huge portable shrine through the streets to a symbolic destination. Such is their exuberance and rapture that real outbreaks of violence can occur. These

At this Yakushiji temple ceremony, priests twirl flaming torches for the crowd.

events have to be seen to be believed: they demonstrate the perfect flip-side of the supposedly reserved Japanese character.

Festivals are where superficially modern Japan gives way to the old, where ancient traditions are upheld, especially in remote rural districts. But there is usually a strong commercial aspect to the celebrations. Some rural communities devise small but colorful festivals to galvanize community spirit and the local economy by attracting badly needed domestic tourists.

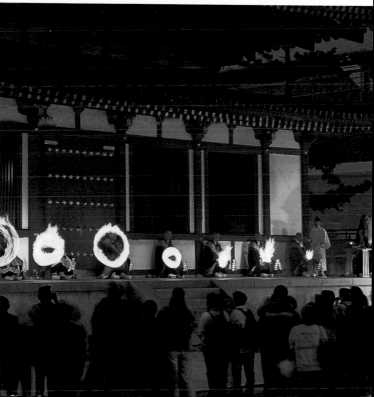

Many festivals, though, are so spectacular that it is worth planning your visit specifically so you can attend. Definitely check with your nearest Japan National Tourist Office for information when planning your trip. Note that since many festivals follow the lunar calendar, the actual dates vary from year to year. With thousands of festivals and ceremonies taking place annually, this entire book wouldn't provide enough space to describe them all. Instead, we offer a sampling of large and small festivals. But when planning a visit, some supplementary research will probably uncover unexpected nuggets.

January. In Japan, New Year's Day is the big festival, closest in spirit to Christmas in the West, the time when relatives and friends pay visits to each other and to the local shrines. New Year's Eve is a quieter, more solemn affair than in the West, when the Japanese flock to famous shrines to pray for good fortune for the coming year. People decorate houses, shops, offices, and even cars with a bouquet of pine and bamboo, symbols of evergreen stability and upright behavior. In Tokyo on 2 January, the

> **During O-bon ("All Souls' Day") the spirits of one's ancestors are believed to return for a brief visit to the family Buddhist altar.**

inner grounds of the Imperial Palace are opened to the public, with thousands coming to pay their respects to the emperor and enjoy a closer peek at his palace than is possible during the rest of the year.

Closet pyromaniacs shouldn't miss Nara's Wakakusayama Turf Burning ceremony on 15 January, when people dressed as warrior monks burn the entire hillside of Mt. Wakakusa after sunset, creating one of the year's most photographed spectacles, visible from miles around. The 15th is also Coming-of-Age Day nationwide, a milestone event for 20-year-olds attaining the age of majority. They attend special ceremonies at local community halls, and women dress in unusually opulent fur-trimmed kimono worn only on this special day.

February. The important *setsubun* festival marks the end of winter around the country on 3–4 February. With demons represented by priests wearing fearsome masks, onlookers throw beans to drive them away while shouting, "Demons out, good fortune in!" The 3rd and 4th are also one of the two occasions each year when the 3,000 lanterns of the Kasuga Grand Shrine in Nara are lit. (The event is repeated on 14–15 August.)

Up in Hokkaido, Sapporo holds its internationally popular Snow Festival (during the first or second week of February). The highlight is an ice sculpture competition at Odori Park, with huge, superbly detailed models of castles, towers, and giant characters both traditional and modern. Throughout Japan, children living in snowy areas look forward each year to the Kamakura Festival, when they build igloo-type snow houses.

Buddhists paying homage to the Kofukuji Buddha triad in Nara.

March. On 3 March is the Hina Doll Festival, a special event for young girls. Exquisitely detailed dolls in ancient costumes representing the imperial couple and other aristocrats are displayed for good luck. Some shrines display thousands of dolls brought by the faithful.

Another annual highlight is the two-week O-Mizu-tori Festival at Nara's Nigatsudo Temple, one of Todaiji's subtemples. Although the central event is a solemn and highly symbolic water-drawing ceremony, the crowds turn out in force for the more public and spectacular fire ceremonies. Every night from the 1st to the 14th, in a highly dramatic display clearly designed to entertain, temple priests brandishing long poles with a flaming cedar ball at each end run along the front of the verandah, deliberately showering the large crowd below with burning embers. (believed to bring good luck for the coming year, having burned away the transgressions from the previous one). In long-exposure photographs of this display, the entire temple appears to be on fire. There is nothing like this anywhere. Photographers: Miss this at your peril!

Another visual treat in March is the annual fertility festival held at Tagata Jinja in Gifu Prefecture, north of Nagoya. This amazing shrine celebrates an object that transcends borders and cultural barriers: the human penis. Phalluses huge and humble, wooden and stone are enshrined and worshipped here. And on 15 March each

year, the mightiest specimen, a 2 m (6.5 ft) monster made of Japanese cypress and weighing over 270 kg (600 pounds) is slowly carried through this small town, bulging out of its portable shrine. See it and you still won't believe it.

On 18 March the Golden Dragon dance is held at Tokyo's Senso-ji Temple (in Asakusa), accompanied by a ceremonial carriage bearing several geisha playing traditional musical instruments.

April. The Buddha's birthday is celebrated with flower festivals held throughout Japan. The best place to view the spring azaleas is at the Azalea Festival in the last week of April at Tokyo's Nezu shrine. In the Kansai region, peony lovers head for Hasedera Temple in rural Nara. April is also cherry blossom season, with blossom-viewing picnics *(hanami)* held in parks and temples throughout Japan as the

At the right time, you can glimpse Japan's fleeting national treasure — cherry blossoms.

cherry-blossom "front" makes its steady progress northward. On the 14th and 15th the city of Takayama in Gifu Prefecture holds one of Japan's greatest processions of large, colorful floats.

May. From the end April and into early May is Golden Week, the unofficial name for the conjunction of three major national holidays (Green Day, Constitution Day, and Children's Day). Since this is the only time many Japanese are permitted to take a vacation, it is the worst time to visit Japan, since every hotel, inn, train, and even plane is booked up months in advance. Although Boys' Day was officially renamed Children's Day to include girls, the reality is taking some time to catch on. This festival features giant carp streamers flying from poles throughout Japan. The carp's ability to struggle upstream against a strong current is regarded as a fit model for Japanese boys.

On 15 May, Kyoto celebrates its Hollyhock Festival (Aoi Matsuri). This ancient ritual is meant to pave the way for a good harvest, with branches of hollyhock to stave off thunder and earthquakes. The hollyhock decorates a big red oxcart, accompanied from the Imperial Gosho Palace by 300 Kyoto citizens dressed in splendid Heian-period costumes.

June. From June onward, *ukai* celebrates the ancient use of cormorant birds to catch *aiyu*, a popular river fish. The animal rights movement has yet to penetrate Japan in any significant way: the cormorants' throats are constricted so they can't swallow the fish they catch underwater, and their owners retrieve the catch when the hapless birds resurface. The various events held around Japan are usually highly ceremonial, with blazing torches illuminating the proceedings.

July. Kyoto's Gion Festival (17–24 July) is the most elaborate procession of the year, with its grandiose floats and glowing lanterns. Originally, the festival invoked the help of the gods against a plague in medieval Kyoto; highly commercialized imitations of it are now celebrated all over the country. Immediately after Gion, on the 24th and 25th, Osaka holds its flamboyant and mammoth Tenjin Matsuri, starting from the Temmangu shrine. It has fireworks, flaming torches, and gaily decorated floats on the central Okawa River.

August. At the height of the summer swelter in July and August is O-bon, a colorful and joyous national Buddhist festival honoring the spirits of deceased ancestors. People travel around the country to clean their family tombs and gravestones. At Nagasaki in mid-August, glowing lanterns decorate the graveyards, while other lanterns are put out to sea on model boats to take the departed souls back to their other world. Like Golden Week in April–May, this is a great time to avoid Japan unless you relish competing for every train seat and hotel bed with millions of others. So bad is the traffic that many of the country's expressways come to a virtual standstill.

On the 14th and 15th of the month is the year's second lighting-up of the thousands of lanterns at Kasuga Grand Shrine in Nara.

Further information. For complete details of these and other major festivals held annually around Japan, check the JNTO website at <www.jnto.go.jp>.

SPORTS

When the Japanese decide to do something, they seem to take a "total-immersion" route, buying the latest outfits and equipment so that they look like seasoned professionals before they take a single lesson. This provides insight into the important Japanese concept of *katachi* (form), the rough equivalent of "It isn't what you do; it's the way that you do it." It is quite common to see Japanese men of all ages standing on train platforms or outside a building practicing their stroke with an imaginary golf club.

Participant Sports

Tennis. With land prices notoriously high, urban courts are crowded and expensive, so your best bet is at the seaside or hot-spring resorts. If necessary, get your hotel to help you make reservations.

Golf. Unsurprisingly, golfing is prohibitively expensive. You will have to share the Japanese golfer's manic obsession to want to shell out green fees of well over US$100 at top clubs during peak periods. The best way to enjoy a round of golf is as the guest of a Japanese friend or business associate.

Swimming. Beaches close to Tokyo and Osaka are crowded (except after 1 September, when summer for the Japanese has officially ended). So you are better off going south to Kyushu, around Shimabara and the more secluded of the Amakusa Islands (for snorkeling and scuba-diving, too) or to the spa resort of Ibusuki. Water sports enthusiasts go south to the beaches of Okinawa, the liveliest being Moon Beach at Nakadomari.

Fishing. One of the joys of fishing in Japan is taking the catch back to your Japanese-style inn and having the cook grill it for you or turn it into sushi or sashimi (depending on your degree of faith in the cleanliness of Japan's highly polluted rivers). Freshwater angling—for bass, carp, or trout—is good anywhere in the lakes and streams, best of all up in Hokkaido, where you stand a decent chance of hooking a salmon. Sea bream and sea bass are the most frequent catch in coastal waters. Ask about license restrictions at the local tourist office.

Skiing. Japan has a number of excellent skiing areas, which quickly get very crowded in season. Winter sports are one of Hokkaido's main draws for domestic tourism, with popular ski resorts at Teine Olympia (outside Sapporo), Niseko, and Kiroro. Others are Zao (in Tohoku) and a number of resorts in Joshin-etsu Kogen National Park in the Japan Alps, where there are now splendid facilities thanks to the 1998 Winter Olympic Games in Nagano.

Spectator Sports

Baseball. The game is at least as popular in Japan as it is in the US. It was introduced in the 19th century, together with railways, cameras, and whisky. Today baseball is big business, with cheerleaders, bal-

Greens of gold—you'll need lots and lots of money if you want to take part in Japan's swinging obsession.

loons, and variations on Major League hype. The major professional teams are owned by the biggest publishing empires or department store chains, each combining their company name with the time-honored American nicknames, the most famous being the Yomiuri Giants. Japanese commentators have happily adopted the American jargon of "Strike one, ball two," "home run," and "pinch hit." In Tokyo you can see games at Korakuen Stadium, and in Osaka at Nissei.

Sumo. Of the traditional Japanese sports, sumo wrestling is the most popular. This ancient sport originated more than 15 centuries ago in Shinto ceremonies. Today, sumo champions—the only men still allowed to wear the samurai warrior's gleaming top-knot hairdo—are national heroes and are much in demand for TV commercials. At the national level, there are a total of 575 wrestlers classed in six divisions according to their win-loss ratio in the annual tour-

Sumo is Japan's most popular spectator sport. The top-ranking wrestlers are idolized like pop stars.

naments. The highest division is the *makuuchi,* of which the champions are known as *yokozuna.* These giants weigh anything from 90 to 165 kg (200 to 350 pounds), yet they have grace, dignity, and suppleness that belie their massive bulk.

The *dohyo-iri* (ring entry) ceremony opening the tournament is a fascinating spectacle. The champions strut into the arena in richly embroidered silk "aprons" covering the solid band protecting their midriffs. In the *dohyo,* a raised mound of hard clay some 4.6 m (15 ft) in diameter under a large suspended Shinto-roof-style canopy, toss salt across the *dohyo* to purify it of evil spirits, swagger around, and commence the all-important "psyching-out" of the opponent. Pointedly avoiding each other's eyes, they raise a massive leg into the air (to a height that would do a professional dancer proud), slam it down with a mighty thud, and lower themselves into the characteristic squat. This goes on for up to five minutes—all part of the great ritual buildup of tension before the wrestlers clash. Note that indulging in these highly stylized opening theatrics is a privilege of top-ranked wrestlers only.

The aim is for one wrestler to force the other out of the ring or to make him touch the floor with anything other than his feet. The bout is usually over in one or two minutes, sometimes mere seconds, but the intensity of the struggle and the sheer visual drama make for compelling entertainment.

Sumo tournaments are held in January, May, and September at the Kuramae Kokugikan in Tokyo, during March in Osaka, in July in Nagoya, and in November in Fukuoka (Kyushu). The bouts commence in the morning, but the real crowds start arriving only in late afternoon. A little known secret is that a standing ticket (usually around US$12) actually gives you the run of the arena: you can move around freely, sit in unoccupied seats, and even enjoy the action from the ringside until the actual ticket-holders arrive later on. If you can, go out of your way to spend a few hours

> **Sumo contestants may not hit below the belt, strike with the closed fist, or pull each other's hair. Otherwise, anything goes.**

of watching live sumo. There is simply nothing on earth like it.

Martial arts. Most major cities have martial arts halls, where you can watch *kendo* (fencing with bamboo staves) as well as the famed sports of judo and aikido. The latter is a highly spiritual art in which, unlike judo, the opponents do not grapple at the beginning of the bout. Instead, they maneuver and feint, applying the strength of their will *(ki)* rather than physical strength to overcome the other.

EATING OUT

I f Japanese culture expresses itself most vividly in its food, that is also where the ultimate adventure for foreign visitors lies. The preparation and presentation of Japanese cuisine reflect the traditional emphasis on form, color, and texture. Any fine Japanese meal is supposed to be a feast for the eyes as well as the palate. The many small bowls and dishes in a typical meal, for instance, are chosen to suit the individual foods they contain.

The secret of enjoying Japanese food is to abandon all preconceptions about what a meal should be and how it should be served. Things you are used to eating hot will be served in Japan at room temperature, and dishes you expect to arrive separately will appear all together—or vice versa. Even people who consider themselves reasonably familiar with Japanese cuisine will find themselves baffled by much of what they encounter in Japan.

This island nation's huge dependence on fish and seafood is famous. Less well known is the fact that Japan has many indigenous vegetables, edible roots, grasses, and even flowers that are simply not found elsewhere. As a result, many meals you are served will contain items that you have never seen before. Tackle these enthusiastically; you are unlikely to find much that is other than wholly delicious. After all, a standard Japanese meal is hardly something from another planet.

A typical traditional meal includes a main dish of cooked chicken, fish, or meat, a few small vegetable dishes, pickles, *miso* (soybean paste) soup, and the ever-present rice. Note that with a *teishoku* (set meal), you order only the main dish by name; the rest comes automatically, which makes things pretty straightforward. However, spare your server or host an interrogation as to the name and nature of every ingredient, many of which have no English equivalent.

Also, don't be offended or intimidated if people stare at you while you're eating. You—as the honorable visitor—are merely

Seaweed specialists—here, harvested wakame seaweed hangs out to dry in the sun.

being observed for signs of approval. Give them a smile and an "Oishii!" ("Delicious!") and you'll make their day.

How to Eat

Don't be daunted by the prospect of arcane rules of etiquette when confronted by your first Japanese dinner, whether formal or casual. The Japanese are taught that their food, like their language, is so impenetrable to outsiders that they consider even the most token effort heroic.

First, we offer a few simple tips. Taking off your shoes before stepping on a *tatami* mat should be obvious. But if you're not comfortable kneeling for long on the floor in the formal Japanese-style, just sit cross-legged like most of the population, especially men. Incidentally, that marvelous wet towel *(oshibori)* you receive to freshen up at the beginning of the meal should be neatly rolled up when you've finished with it. Don't, however, use it on anything except your hands.

Eating with chopsticks involves resting the inside stick firmly against the hand while moving the other like a pen to grasp your

Grilled squid makes a tasty and traditional midday snack—a hot favorite at outdoor festivals and events.

prey. However badly you cope, don't be surprised when your Japanese friends compliment you profusely—another admirable effort by their esteemed guest.

When drinking beer or *sake* (or anything else) with companions, you should serve your neighbor but not serve yourself, even if you have your own little jug in front of you. Your host will insist on doing the honors. Always hold your cup or glass when someone is pouring for you, to show your appreciation. For soup, take the small items of food using your chopsticks and drink the broth directly from the bowl, as there'll be no spoon. Make all the noise you like; it's not only expected but considered a compliment to the chef. Most Japanese slurp loudly when eating noodles, sucking them in with gusto. The extra intake of oxygen is said to improve the taste—but novice slurpers should beware of hyperventilating.

Where to Eat

The high-class places *(ryotei)* serving Japanese haute cuisine live up to their international reputation for being eye-wateringly expensive. Given the meticulous preparation and the quality of the ingredients, the prices are perhaps justifiable. Generally, though, they are for the well-to-do and for businessmen on expense accounts. Nevertheless, you should consider budgeting for at least one elaborate Japanese dinner in a fine restaurant—many of which serve excellent food at more reasonable prices.

One economical way to do this is to stay at a traditional Japanese inn *(ryokan),* where the price usually includes a superb dinner followed by an equally impressive breakfast the next morning. If you're lucky enough to have time to explore Japan beyond the confines of Tokyo, consider saving for a fine meal in one of the great gourmet centers such as Kyoto or Osaka or the major towns of Kyushu. There, you'll be sampling regional delicacies at their freshest while avoiding paying the premium of eating in Japan's most expensive city.

Sushi to last forever—these plastic replicas might keep longer than fresh sushi, but they cost more than the real thing.

But more than most countries, Japan is blessed with excellent small, modestly priced restaurants serving typical Japanese food of very high quality. Many of these have a single specialty, as evidenced in the establishment's name: *sushi-ya, yakitori-ya,* or *okonomiyaki-ya.* All have a short cloth curtain *(noren)* over the door; if it's fluttering outside, they are open. Even if you can't read the writing on the sign, many advertise their fare with a window display of astonishingly realistic plastic replicas of the food served within. These imitations of meat, fish, vegetables, rice, and noodles are a great help in ordering your meal. If the menu has no explanation in English, just step outside again with the waiter and point to what you want.

If you don't want to restrict yourself to one particular cuisine, try an *izakaya.* Often called Japanese "pubs," these are really restaurants catering to enthusiastic drinkers rather than bars with food. *Izakaya* are lively, informal restaurants offering a bit of everything: sushi, *tempura*, *yakitori*, cooked fish, vegetables, and salads, as well as strange interpretations of Western sundries such as chips and pizza. *Izakaya* are usually packed to overflowing on Friday nights, when the nation's increasingly pressured office workers go out with friends or co-workers.

Lowest on the social rung but no less worthy of your business are the street pushcarts *(yatai)* serving roasted sweet potatoes, *ramen* noodles in soup, stewed vegetables *(oden)*, or grilled chicken. With a little roof to keep off the rain and stools for the customers, the ven-

Plastic Fantastic

All visitors to Japan will soon notice the deliciously realistic models of meals featured in restaurant windows. The manufacture of these plastic replicas is a whole industry in itself. It dates back to the Meiji Restoration of 1868, when the Japanese had to explain with models made of wax the new foods coming in from abroad.

Today's factories employ professional cooks to regulate the size, shape, and color of the "food" to be made out of various vinyl resins. It has proved impossible for artisans other than real sushi cooks to compose convincing replicas of the little oblongs of raw fish on rice, but most ordinary craftsmen can manage a bowl of noodles all by themselves. Art students do the painting, and women assemble the finished product on its dish.

You can buy one of these "meals" as a souvenir; they certainly last longer than the real thing. The factories' sales outlets are located in neighborhoods specializing in restaurant equipment, such as Asakusa in Tokyo and Doguyu-suji in Osaka's Namba. The results are astonishingly realistic — but these tasty tidbits don't come cheap.

dors set up shop in entertainment districts such as Tokyo's Kabuki-cho and Asakusa and Osaka's Shinsaibashi, or around major railway stations, doing their best business late at night.

In a separate category, *kissaten* are small coffee shops found absolutely everywhere. Before 11am, the price of a cup of coffee usually gets you a simple breakfast *(mohningu saabisu)* comprising a slice of toast, a hard-boiled egg, and sometimes a mini salad. Throughout the day they also serve sandwiches, cakes, and snacks.

In Japan, "take-out" food can come in the form of the home-grown version of the packed lunch: the neat little box *(bento)* containing rice with fish or meat and various elegantly presented vegetable concoctions. In fact, so important is the *bento* in daily life that generations of mothers have traditionally competed to outdo each other with the boxes they prepare for their children and husbands.

What to Eat

With only a few exceptions, cooked food is usually served warm rather than hot. The Japanese don't feel it loses its flavor if you let it get cold while sampling something else, since many dishes are served simultaneously. Japanese rice is short grain and specially bred to be sticky (quite different from the "dry" long-grain rice favored in the West).

Breakfast

Although you might not welcome a Japanese-style breakfast every morning, do try it at least once. Not only is it low-fat, healthy, and delicious, but it sustains you remarkably well for another day of arduous sightseeing. Since a traditional breakfast is not generally available in restaurants and coffee shops, Japanese inns are your best bet. The full version is likely to include grilled salted fish served at room temperature, hot *miso* soup with a few vegetables and *tofu* (high-protein white bean-curd), a bowl of rice, and tea.

Good to look at, even better to eat! A traditional Japanese dinner with all the trimmings is an adventure in itself.

Lunch and Dinner

One of the most popular Japanese lunches is *soba* (brown buckwheat noodles) served in a fish-based broth with a wide variety of added extras including fried beancurd, leeks, mushrooms, fish, chicken, and other vegetables. One bowl makes a fine meal in the middle of a busy day. The thicker white noodles are called *udon,* and the yellow curly Chinese ones *shinasoba*. Noodles may also be served cold *(zaru-soba or zaru-udon),* accompanied by a tasty soy-based dipping sauce to which you add fresh chopped onions, ginger, and fiery *wasabi* (Japanese horseradish).

Udon is also served in a stew *(nabe)* containing fish, meat, or chicken with vegetables and *tofu,* usually served in a cast-iron or heavy ceramic pot. A *nabe* is an informal traditional winter dish that is often shared by a group of people.

Another popular lunch staple is the *donburi:* a bowl of rice topped with a savory mixture of cooked egg, onion, soy sauce, and a main ingredient, usually a breaded pork cutlet *(tonkatsu,* another national institution), chicken, or vegetables.

Donburi and noodle dishes occupy most of the window space in restaurants around the country serving lunches and light meals, so it's a good idea to get acquainted with them at an early stage.

Worth the wait...Customers line up for bowls of steaming hot ramen noodles.

Another keyword with which to arm yourself for lunch is the *teishoku,* which simply means "set meal." The main dish you order comes with vegetables, rice soup, and pickles, a format which provides the best value meals in Japan. Restaurants located in the busy commercial centers of cities compete fiercely to attract office workers at lunchtime, and amazing bargains can be found as long as you can get a seat. (Try after 1pm to avoid the crowds.)

Sashimi, usually served as a choice item within a larger meal, is premium raw fish sliced in bite-size pieces. It's dipped in a sauce you prepare to your own degree of spiciness from *wasabi* (mustard-like green horseradish—a little goes a long way), *shisonomi* herb-buds and soy sauce. The most common fish is **¢**na: *maguro* is the deep-red meat and

> A certain amount of noise is expected when you eat noodle dishes like soba and ramen. It's not impolite to slurp.

toro the richer pink parts. Others are *tai* (sea bream), *sake* (salmon, but pronounced "sha-keh"), *hamachi* (mackerel), and *aji* (pompano).

Sushi comes in two main types: *nigiri-zushi* is raw fish and (usually) boiled seafood on top of a patty of cold rice cooked with a little diluted vinegar to hold it together in an oblong shape. *Maki-zushi* are seaweed rolls, skinny or fat, filled with any combination of raw fish, seafood, vegetables, and pickles.

The seafood used reflects the astonishing bounty of the teeming waters surrounding Japan: octopus, squid, clams, scallops, prawns, and shrimps. When eating, try to turn the sushi upside down in the soy sauce so that only the fish is dipped; otherwise, the rice disintegrates—a classic novice error. In sushi bars, you sit at a table with a selection of assorted fish and seafood. If you're not sure what specifically to order, ask for a selection; several combinations are always available at different prices.

Much more fun, though, is to sit where the real action is: up at the counter. Here you can choose the ingredients you want to try just by pointing (with a quick "Sumimasen!" for "Excuse me!"), then watch the sushi chef's dexterity as he deftly slices to create just the right shape (the result of years of training). Wash down your sushi with beer, cold or hot *sake*, or hot tea.

Sukiyaki (pronounced "ski-yaki") was introduced only in the 19th century after the arrival of Americans demanding beef. Beginning as a characteristically inspired attempt to imitate—and ultimately surpass—the sailors' beef stew, the thin slices of tender beef are sautéed before you over a gas or charcoal fire. The meat is then stirred with translucent vermicelli, finely shredded green onions, mushrooms, and greens (spinach or other green leaves). All the ingredients are appetizingly set out on a board beforehand. Tastiest by far is the fabled beef from Kobe: to give it flavor and keep it tender, the cattle are fed beer and lovingly massaged before being turned into beef.

For a do-it-yourself meal, try *shabu-shabu,* sliced thinly beef which you boil in a pot set in front of you with chicken stock, cabbage, carrots, spinach, mushrooms, and *tofu.*

Okonomiyaki is a very cheap do-it-yourself meal, especially popular with students and other young people. It's a Japanese-style savory pancake containing chopped cabbage in an egg-based batter to which you add shrimp, squid, meat, or other ingredients. The whole thing is then prepared on the hot griddle built into your table. Someone is always on hand to show you how. As well as being great fun, an *okonomiyaki* or two can make a tasty lunch or dinner.

> **The best tempura is only lightly battered, dry, and crispy—one of the few Japanese foods that must be served piping hot.**

A warming winter favorite, *oden* is an informal hearty selection of stewed items more often sold by street vendors than by restaurants. You'll find everything stewing in the kelp-and-fish based broth: squid, seaweed, Japanese radish, potatoes, hard-boiled eggs, *tofu,* and various meaty morsels.

Yakitori are wooden skewers with pieces of chicken barbecued and served with a savory sauce. Various combinations of chicken

Skewered cubes of chicken and veg on a stick, yakitori makes the perfect light meal, with "Cup" sake to wash it down.

parts, green onions, mushrooms, and other vegetables are usually on the menu. *Yakitori* makes a great informal light dinner, usually with plenty of beer to wash it down. These lively, informal restaurants almost always feature a distinctive row of small red lanterns outside.

Tempura is a famous example of the Japanese transforming a foreign import into a unique and wholly original creation—in this case, Portuguese fritters prepared by the missionaries *ad tempora)*. A typical selection includes a prawn or two, a mushroom, a small green pepper, and slices of other vegetables, all coated in a light batter of egg and flour, deep fried, and decoratively served along with a dipping sauce to which you then add grated radish and ginger.

If you have the chance, try *robatayaki,* which is simply anything you choose grilled in front of you on a large *robata* grill: fish, meat, seafood, and numerous vegetables. Being able to point at whatever you want transcends the language barrier. *Robatayaki* restaurants tend to have traditional rural décor and are usually atmospheric venues.

One of the world's supreme snack foods is the *onigiri,* a brilliant invention comprising a small triangle (or ball) of rice containing a filling of shredded salted salmon, seaweed, fish roe, or any of countless other ingredients, all enclosed in a wrapping of *nori* (seaweed). These are sold in the convenience stores which seem to adorn every main street; one or two are ideal for restoring the energy of fading tourists. Note the ingenious multistage packaging separating the dry *nori* from the rice ball inside.

Despite the unfamiliarity of much of what you encounter, Japan has very few dishes that will shock a typical Western palate. For example, the Japanese (unlike many other Asians) are very conservative when it comes to meat, chicken, and fish, discarding all but the choicest morsels. Don't worry about not knowing what something is; just dig in and enjoy!

Desserts

Traditional Japanese meals do not end with a dessert course. However, the Japanese definitely have a sweet tooth, as any visit to a coffee shop or department store will confirm. There you will find an amazing variety of Western-style cakes, pastries, fancy cookies, and biscuits.

More interesting, though, is the seemingly infinite range of indigenous confections. Many of these are based on sticky rice and sweet red bean paste (with lots of added sugar) and fall somewhere between the categories of sweets and cakes. *Wagashi* is made from wheat or rice flour, mashed red beans, yams, arrowroot, egg, and sugar. The moist sweets are known as *yokan,* a bean-paste jelly served in long rectangles and sliced. *Manju* are very popular sweet rice dumplings filled with red bean paste. All of these are very commonly given as gifts to friends and associates, as the exquisite department store displays (and prices) imply.

Savory snacks are also very popular, especially *senbei,* the famous Japanese rice crackers that come in all shapes, sizes, and flavors.

The Japanese absolutely hated milk when the Americans first suggested getting it from a cow, and ice cream has never caught up with Western standards. However, there is one interesting innovation in this domain: *matcha-aisu-kurii-mu,* or ice cream flavored with green tea.

What to Drink

Whisky is considered the sophisticated alcoholic drink by middle-class upwardly mobile Japanese, although sake remains the national alcoholic beverage par excellence. Sake ranges from seriously rough stuff sold in machines to splendidly subtle creations prized by connoisseurs around the country. A colorless wine fermented from rice, it is drunk from thimble-sized cups. Heating actually

Elaborately decorated barrels are used to store sake, Japan's famous rice wine.

More than Just a Cup of Tea

Nothing expresses Japanese formalism and emphasis on social protocol more effectively than the tea ceremony. As you travel around Japan, you might have a chance to participate in a simple tea ceremony at a Zen Buddhist temple in Kamakura or Kyoto, at a teahouse in one of the "strolling" gardens, or even in special rooms at your hotel.

The earliest Zen Buddhist monks drank the slightly bitter green tea in order to stay awake while meditating—green tea is high in both vitamin C and caffeine. Today's elegant tea ceremony was refined in the 15th century to induce the mental tranquillity necessary to continue along the path toward religious enlightenment. The tea itself was not the point. Rather, the emphasis lay in the protocol, ritual, and resulting atmosphere associated with every single aspect of its preparation.

Over the centuries, the ceremony has accumulated exquisitely designed utensils: bowls, tea kettle, tea caddy, hot water jug, miniature brazier, a long, slender scoop for the tea powder, and a little whisk for mixing it. A scroll is hung in an alcove, together with an exquisite ikebana flower arrangement.

If you are served first, be sure to bow to the host and then turn to your neighbor and say "Excuse me for drinking before you." Take the bowl with your right hand and rest it on the palm of your left, turning the bowl's decorative pattern away from you for others to admire.

Sip the tea loudly, then wipe the bowl's edge and turn its decorative pattern to admire it yourself. Expressing admiration for the tea bowls, utensils, and other objects of definitively understated beauty is an important aspect of the proceedings. The ceremony is finished when the host removes the tea caddy and scoop.

destroys many of the subtle, fleeting flavors of the finest sake, which is usually consumed chilled.

Fruit-flavored cocktails are also popular, mostly based on *shochu,* a family of dry vodka-like spirits distilled from ingredients such as potatoes and grains. A highly potent example is Kyushu's *imo jochu,* distilled from sweet potatoes.

The Japanese are massive consumers of beer, especially German-style lager, which has been produced ever since a German visited Hokkaido in the 1870s and found it ideal for growing hops. The big breweries battle it out in a fiercely competitive market by launching seasonal brews featuring differing flavors and alcohol content (the latter indicated on the side of the can or bottle label).

Finally, the ubiquitous tea. Green tea *(o-cha)* is green because it is unfermented; it was originally introduced from China. The green tea powder is prepared in lukewarm water, and only the finest quality is used in the tea ceremony. *Sencha* is the common variety of tea leaves, while *bancha* (the kind served in sushi bars and small restaurants) is coarser and requires boiling water. Last of all is *hojicha,* a brown tea with a nice smoky tang to it, also brewed using boiling water.

However, many so-called teas actually contain no tea leaves at all, brewed instead from herbs and grains. These are usually very healthy and are served cold in the summer and hot in the winter. Many of the unidentifiable drinks you see in Japanese vending machines are herb or grain teas. To beat the summer heat, try cold *mugi-cha,* made from barley.

Western-Style Food

However much you love Japanese food, you might get a craving for something more familiar. The major Western-style hotels have both Western and Japanese menus. In most cities and towns you will find no shortage of establishments claiming to offer such international fare as Indian, French, Italian, and Chinese. But be forewarned: such food is usually highly modified to suit the local palate. Anyone used

A simple, elegant Kyoto restaurant sets the tone for a simple, elegant meal.

to Chinese food in, say, Hong Kong or even the US is unlikely to be impressed by what is served in Japan. Italian and French fare has become enormously popular, especially among the young, but you should again expect to be disappointed. The dishes you are served might look authentic, but somehow they never taste quite right. (They are also often served in annoyingly small portions.)

As for sandwiches: forget it—except as an emergency last resort. Despite Japan's long record of dramatically improving on imported concepts, the Japanese sandwich is a veritable disaster, with dainty, crustless slices of fluffy white bread providing only a token hint of whatever is supposed to be inside. And at convenience stores, only the truly open-minded will sample such culinary horrors as the fried noodle roll or the fruit salad and whipped cream sandwich.

INDEX

HANDY TRAVEL TIPS

An A–Z Summary of Practical Information

> *Note:* To telephone Japan from abroad, always dial the country code (81) and then the appropriate city code, followed by the number. If you are in Japan, a 0 precedes the city code when dialing from one city to another; the 0 is not necessary when calling from outside Japan (see TELEPHONE).

A

ACCOMMODATIONS

A wide variety of accommodation is available in Japan, ranging from international-class Western-style hotels to Buddhist temples. During the Japanese holidays (see holidays) early reservations are essential. If you are stuck without a room, contact an office of the Japan Travel Bureau (JNTO), where you will be able to find help.

Western-style hotels. Most of the international hotels belong to the Japan Hotel Association. They are comparable to equivalent hotels in Europe or the US and offer Western-style facilities and cuisine, although Japanese food is also available. Rates may be reduced under certain circumstances (off season, long stay, group discount). Reservations can be made through any travel agent and certain airlines, or by contacting the hotel directly.

Japanese-style inns *(ryokan)*. For a more informal atmosphere and a taste of the Japanese way of life, stay at a traditional inn. These vary from large hotel-scale establishments to small, hospitable, family-run hotels. Reservations can be made through a travel agent or through the inn itself. Prices are always per person (rather than per room) and almost always include a sumptuous dinner and breakfast featuring regional specialties. Guest rooms are Japanese-style, with *tatami*-mat floors and a cotton *futon* as a bed. En-suite bathrooms are only sometimes available, but most *ryokan* feature private use of a Japanese-style hot tub. The rate is sometimes reduced by 10% to 20% if meals are omitted, but this should always be agreed before checking in. Check-in time is usually between 3pm and 4 pm, check-out time from 10am to 11 am.

There are some 80,000 *ryokan,* about 2,000 of which belong to the Japan Ryokan Association. The Japanese Inn Group is a network of independent and very reasonably priced *ryokan* providing a warm and friendly way to experience Japanese-style lodging.

Guesthouses *(minshuku).* This is another type of Japanese-style accommodation, often located in holiday resorts. The guest is treated as a member of the family. The per-person charge only sometimes includes dinner and breakfast, and you are expected to lay out your bedding at night and roll it up and stow it away again the next morning.

The Japan National Tourist Organization (JNTO) recommends about 300 *minshuku* for foreign visitors. Welcome Inn Reservation Center offers a free reservation service at a wide range of *minshuku* and *ryokan* that charge not more than ¥8,000 per night per person. Reservation request forms are available at JNTO overseas offices. Note that the Welcome Inn service now strictly requires reservations at least three weeks in advance. Highly recommended and much more flexible are the 70 member inns of the Japanese Inn Group (Asakusa Shigetsu Ryokan, 1-31-11 Asakusa, Taito-ku, Tokyo 111-0032; Tel: 03/3843-2345; fax 03/3843-2348).

Home-stay system. If you want to learn more about typical Japanese home life first-hand, you can stay with a Japanese family via the Japanese Association of the Experiment in International Living (EIL Japan), which organizes stays of one to four weeks. You need to apply to an EIL office six to eight weeks in advance. In the UK, contact the EIL, 287 Worcester Road, Malvern, Worcestershire WR14 4EN; Tel. (01684) 562577, fax (01684) 562212. In the US, contact World Learning, P.O. Box 676, Brattleboro, VT 05346; Tel. 802-257-7751.

Buddhist temples *(shukubo).* Anyone may stay at one of the many Japanese temples offering surprisingly luxurious accommodations, in the tradition of temples offering accommodation to wandering pilgrims. These provide a glimpse into the monks' daily life and routines. Food is usually strictly vegetarian and even sumptuous. Guests are sometimes expected to help with some light chores and may attend early morning prayer services. Reservations can be made through the JNTO, which can provide full details. The greatest concentration of *shukubo* is in the mountain-top Buddhist enclave of Koyasan in Wakayama.

AIRPORTS

Tokyo's airport at Narita and Kansai International Airport near Osaka are Japan's two main air gateways. However, there are also international airports at Nagoya, Fukuoka, and Okinawa, and a few international flights use Hiroshima, Oita, Okayama, Kagoshima, Kumamoto, Nagasaki, Komatsu, Kanazawa, Niigata, Sendai, Takamatsu, and Sapporo airports.

Narita. New Tokyo International Airport (Narita) is almost 60 km (37 miles) east of the city center. Access to Tokyo is by limousine, bus, train or taxi; tickets for all downtown transfers can be purchased in the airport arrival lobby. Buses depart at frequent intervals for the Tokyo City Air Terminal and numerous other major points around Tokyo (travel time around 60 minutes) and Yokohama (90 minutes). Travel time is heavily dependent on traffic conditions. If you have a meeting or a flight to catch, assume the worst and allow plenty of extra time for traffic. The bus has long been the standard airport link; only the fattest expense accounts can bear the cost of the trip to or from Tokyo in a Japanese taxi. There is also a bus link with Haneda, Tokyo's main domestic airport, taking around 75 minutes.

Various trains are also available, operated by Japan Railways (JR) and Keisei Railways. These are faster and more reliable, since they avoid Tokyo's notorious traffic. All services take 60 to 90 minutes to or from central Tokyo depending on the service. In Narita, the train platforms are located underground below the terminal buildings. The JR Narita Express goes to Shinjuku, Ikebukuro, Ofuna, and Yokohama via Tokyo Station. The less-expensive Keisei Skyliner Train leaves from the Keisei station in Ueno and arrives at the Keisei Airport Station (just 6 minutes from the airport by shuttle bus). Finally, an Airport Limited Express train service links Narita with Haneda Airport; that journey takes about one hour 45 minutes.

A taxi from Narita to the center of Tokyo can take 90 minutes or more, depending on traffic conditions. Inter-airport transfer to Tokyo Haneda Airport by limousine bus takes 1 hour 40 minutes.

NOTE: Passengers flying from Narita have to pay an airport departure tax of ¥2,040.

Haneda. Tokyo Haneda is the city's second airport, serving mainly domestic routes. It is 20 km (12.5 miles) south of the city center. Transport to town is by monorail to Hamamatsu-cho Station (departure every 6 minutes, travel time 15 minutes).

Kansai. Kansai International Airport (Osaka) is situated southeast of the city center on Osaka Bay. A comprehensive network of limousine buses leave every 20 minutes or so from main points around Osaka (travel time around 45 minutes), including Umeda and Namba stations, as well as from Kobe, Nara, and other locations throughout Kansai. You can also take the Nankai "Rapito" express train from the Nankai station in Namba, the JR Airport Express from Kyobashi, or JR's Haruka express train from Kyoto.

Nagoya. Nagoya International Airport (Komaki) is just 17 km (10.5 miles) from that city. Coaches leave every 15 minutes for Nagoya railway station; the city bus leaves every 30 minutes (journey time about 40 minutes).

B

BUDGETING for YOUR TRIP

To give you an idea of what to expect, here is a list of average prices in Japanese yen (¥). However, they can only be approximate, as inflation creeps relentlessly higher here as elsewhere. A consumption tax of 5 percent is added to most goods and services.

Airport transfer. Narita to Tokyo City Air Terminal: ¥2,700. Narita to JR Tokyo Station: ¥2,800. Narita to Keisei Ueno Station (Skyliner train): ¥1,740. Narita to Haneda Airport (limousine bus): ¥2,900. Narita to Yokohama City Air Terminal (limousine bus): ¥3,300.

Japan

Car rental. (average daily rates with unlimited mileage) economy: ¥8,000–¥9,000; compact: ¥12,000–¥18,000; mid-size: ¥21,000–¥27,000; full-size: ¥29,000–¥35,000. Weekly and monthly rates are also available.

Cigarettes. Japanese brands ¥220–¥260; imported brands ¥300–¥330.

Guides. ¥17,000–¥30,000 per day (half-day rates are also available).

Barbers and hairdressers. Hotels: haircut ¥3,800; shave ¥2,800; shampoo ¥3,100.

Hotels (double room with private bath). Western-style, per room: ¥10,000–¥45,000 daily. *Ryokan* (including 2 meals, per person): ¥10,000¥40,000 daily (rates often vary for busy and off-peak seasons). *Minshuku* (including 2 meals): ¥5,000–¥8,000 daily.

Meals. In a moderately priced restaurant, a Western meal will cost from ¥3,000 to ¥10,000 (steak is expensive, but most other Western dishes are cheaper) and a Japanese meal will cost between ¥5,000 and ¥15,000. A self-service meal ranges from ¥800 to ¥3,000.

Nightclubs. In most nightclubs there's a cover charge (¥3,000 and up) and a hostess charge (¥30,000–¥60,000 for 2 hours), plus service and tax, which means an evening's entertainment can cost as much as ¥130,000.

Taxi. Fares in Tokyo are around ¥660 for the first 2 km (1.25 miles); elsewhere in Japan the fare is ¥550–¥610. Add ¥90 for each additional 347 m (1,140 yards), plus a time charge if the taxi is moving at less than 10 km/hr. From 11pm to 5am the fare is increased by 30 percent.

Public transportation. *Bus:* in Tokyo the single fare on all routes is ¥180; in other towns a flat rate of ¥160–¥200 is charged on most routes. For longer journeys the fare is calculated depending on the distance traveled. Long-distance coach: Tokyo–Nagoya (6 hr) ¥5,500; Tokyo–Kyoto (8 hr) ¥8,050; Tokyo–Osaka (8 hr 45 min) ¥8,450. *Subway:* Tokyo minimum fare ¥160, Osaka ¥200. *Train:* A first-class rail pass is ¥37,000 for 7 days, ¥60,000 for 14 days, ¥78,000 for 21 days. An ordinary-class rail pass: ¥27,800 for 7 days, ¥44,200 for 14 days, ¥56,600 for 21 days. Children aged 6–11 pay half-price.

C

CAMPING

There are various camping sites throughout the country. For details, contact the Japan Auto Camping Association (New Ueno Bldg., 7th floor, 1-24 Yotsuya, Shinjuku-ku, Tokyo; Tel. 03/3357-2851). The Tourist Information Centers (TIC) in Tokyo (Yurakucho) and Kyoto (in the Kyoto Tower) provide details of reservations and costs and can supply a map of Japan showing the camping sites. Camping on private land is sometimes possible, but you must obtain prior permission from the owner.

 Experienced campers might want to stay in the public lodgings *(kokumin shukusha)* built in scenic places or national park areas and operated by the Ministry of Health and Welfare. Lodging includes two meals. Reservations should be made through a TIC or directly with the lodging.

CAR RENTAL

There are car rental firms in all major cities. Except for holders of US and Canadian driving licenses, an International Driving Permit is required. It is possible to rent a car with an English-speaking driver, either through your hotel or a travel agent.

CLIMATE

Japan has four dramatically distinct seasons — although many Japanese feel the rainy season lasting from mid-June to early July should also be counted. There is a vast difference between the subarctic north and the subtropical south, and the climate varies considerably according to region and season.

January and February are the ideal months for winter sports, when most of the country north of Osaka lies under a blanket of snow. March, April, and May are cherry blossom time: warm and sunny. From mid-June to mid-July is the rainy season, followed by hot, jungle-like humidity during August and September. Unless you enjoy your clothes sticking to you from dawn till dusk, this is a good time to avoid Japan, since walking around is essential for sightseeing. September usually brings strong winds, more rain, and typhoons, followed by clear skies and bright sunshine during the autumn months.

Weather is definitely a popular and ongoing topic for conversation throughout the year, especially the rain, which can be unpredictable much of the time. For this reason, a sturdy collapsible umbrella is an essential accessory for the savvy traveler.

Average monthly temperatures in Tokyo:

	J	F	M	A	M	J	J	A	S	O	N	D
Maximum°F	46	48	54	63	72	76	83	86	79	70	60	52
Maximum°C	8	9	12	17	22	24	28	30	26	21	16	11
Minimum °F	29	31	36	46	54	63	70	72	66	55	43	33
Minimum°C	-2	-1	2	8	12	17	21	22	19	13	6	1

CLOTHING

The Japanese have conservative tastes in clothing. Dress is slowly changing both in the workplace and in social settings (but most businessmen still wear dark suits, white shirts, and ill-fitting shoes). As a result, subdued colors and subtle designs are preferable — at least if you don't want to stand out too much.

Your wardrobe should be versatile, lightweight, and easy to wash. Be sure to pack a raincoat. Extra-warm sweaters and a warm coat are necessary in winter. You should avoid tight, restrictive clothing: remember that you will often be seated at low tables with your legs folded underneath you or crossed — not easy in a tight skirt. Remember also that your socks will often be on view and you'll be embarrassed if your toes are poking through holes for all to see; temple floors can be very cold, so pack at least one pair of thick woolly socks. You will have to take your shoes off so often that you will be glad to wear slip-ons. A good pair of comfortable walking shoes is useful for sightseeing, as Japanese paths are graveled and hard.

If you want to buy clothes in Japan, be forewarned that both men's and women's clothing is designed for Japanese body shapes, which are different from those of most Westerners. Also, Japanese underwear generally does not suit Western builds. However, Western-sized clothes are gradually becoming more available in Tokyo and other major cities.

CRIME and SAFETY

The crime rate in Japan is extremely low; it is unlikely that you will be attacked or robbed. However, Japan's is by no means a crime-free society, and all categories of crime — including sexual assault and other violent crimes — are rising steadily. As when traveling anywhere in the world, sensible precautions are recommended. In Tokyo and other large cities, small neighborhood police boxes (called *koban,* easily identifiable with their large red lamp above the door) are located at most major street junctions (see POLICE).

CUSTOMS and ENTRY REGULATIONS

To enter Japan, you will need a valid passport, and you will have to fill in an embarkation/disembarkation card. On arrival you may be asked to show your return ticket and prove you have the means to support yourself during your stay.

Visas. Tourists from the UK and Ireland do not need a visa if they intend to stay less than 180 days in Japan. Americans, Canadians, and New Zealanders may stay 90 days without a visa; visitors from Australia can obtain a free visa from a Japanese consulate or embassy before leaving home. Tourists from South Africa can obtain a visa from a Japanese embassy before leaving home and can stay up to 90 days. Any visitor staying more than 90 days must apply at the local Japanese police station or city hall for an Alien Registration Certificate.

Customs regulations. Officially, goods you bring into Japan should be declared either orally or in writing. However, Japan has now adopted the customs clearance system of spot-checking practiced in many other countries. There is no limit on the amount of currency you can bring into the country. You can take out up to ¥5 million; if you should want to take out more, you must obtain permission from the Ministry of Finance. Certain fresh fruits and vegetables may not be imported into Japan. Certain stimulants found in Western medicines are prohibited as well.

D

DRIVING (see also CAR RENTAL)

The difficulties of driving in Japan shouldn't be underestimated. Driving standards vary greatly, and Japanese roads seem to have more than their fair share of speed demons and people with zero observation skills. As a result, traffic accidents, injuries, and fatalities keep breaking records. For visitors, defensive and cautious driving is essential.

Traffic keeps to the left — which won't worry British drivers — but almost all visitors from abroad will find the traffic conditions daunting. The streets are congested, and parking is highly restricted. The greatest challenge to navigating is the fact that very few streets have names. Instead, building blocks are numbered based on an archaic system; most streets simply serve to separate the blocks. Most traffic signs are written in both roman and Japanese characters.

Speed limits are 40 km/hr (25 mph) in towns, 60 km/hr (38 mph) in suburbs, and 100 km/hr (63 mph) on expressways.

Fluid measures

Distance

The Japanese Automobile Federation (Tel. 03/3436-2811) publishes an English-language guide to driving in Japan entitled *Rules of the Road*. Japan's drunk-driving laws are very severe —the legal limit is zero — but drinking is so commonplace and traffic police so few and far between than late-night driving in cities should be avoided when at all possible.

E

ELECTRICITY

The current is 100 volts throughout Japan, with 50 cycles in Tokyo and eastern Japan and 60 cycles in western Japan (including Nagoya, Kyoto, and Osaka). However, most modern appliances are designed to handle both, so this discrepancy is rarely a problem. American-style flat-pin plugs and outlets are used; non-Americans wishing to use their own appliances will need an adapter and, if necessary, a transformer. Major hotels have 110- and 220-volt outlets for razors, hairdryers, and other appliances.

EMBASSIES

Australia: 1-14 Mita 2-chome, Minato-ku, Tokyo; Tel. (03) 5232-4008.

Canada: 3-38 Akasaka 7-chome, Minato-ku, Tokyo; Tel. (03) 3408-2108.

New Zealand: 20-40 Kamiyama-cho, Shibuya-ku, Tokyo; Tel. (03) 3467-2271.

UK: 1 Ichiban-cho, Chiyoda-ku, Tokyo; Tel. (03) 3265-4001.

US: 10-5 Akasaka l-chome, Minato-ku, Tokyo; Tel. (03) 3224-5128.

EMERGENCIES

Dial 110 for police and 119 for an ambulance or the fire department. In case of illness, you should notify the hotel desk immediately. For hospital information in Tokyo, call (03) 3212-2323. (See also EMBASSIES, HEALTH and MEDICAL CARE, and POLICE.)

G

GAY and LESBIAN TRAVELERS

Japan is not particularly hostile to homosexuality, although it is not a life-choice asserted or celebrated as openly as it is in some Western cultures. Visitors might find the gay and lesbian nightlife scene a little difficult to discover and negotiate. The best-known quarter in Tokyo is Shinjuku 2-chome, but there are clubs, discos, and drag bars in Roppongi and other areas as well. A useful resource is the magazine *Out in Japan,* available at English-language bookstores.

GETTING THERE

From the UK. Daily flights depart to Tokyo and Kansai from London's Heathrow and Gatwick airports. Nonstop flights take 12 hours.

From North America. There are several daily nonstop flights from New York, Los Angeles, San Francisco, and many other cities. Round-the-world fares are available, which allow flights first to Europe and then on to the East Asia, returning directly to North America. This fare is designed for those who wish to stop en route in Europe.

From Australia. Direct flights run daily from Sydney to Tokyo, taking about 9 hours.

GUIDES and TOURS

To help visitors, the Japan National Tourist Organization (JNTO) has inaugurated a "goodwill guide" service. These voluntary guides — there are more than 35,000 of them — can easily be recognized by the distinctive badges they wear. They are happy to answer questions, give directions, and assist in any other way they can.

If you need the services of a professional guide for sightseeing, shopping, or business purposes, you can arrange for one through major travel agents or the Japan Guide Association (Shin-Kokusai Bldg., 3-4-1 Marunouchi, Chiyoda-ku, Tokyo; Tel. 03/3213-2706). This organization can provide guides who speak English, French, Italian, Spanish, Portuguese, German, Russian, Chinese, or Korean.

H

HEALTH and MEDICAL CARE

For minor ailments, your hotel or local Tourist Information Center (TIC) can contact an English-speaking doctor. Hospitals with English-speaking staff include St. Luke's International Hospital, the International Catholic Hospital, and the Japanese Red Cross Medical Center in Tokyo; the Bluff Hospital in Yokohama; the Baptist Hospital and the Sorabe Clinic in Kyoto; the Sumitomo Hospital and the Yodogawa Christian Hospital in Osaka; and the Kaisci Hospital and the Kobe Adventist Clinic in Kobe. For hospital information in Tokyo, dial 3212-2323.

Although you will find a large selection of imported medicines and toiletries at the American Pharmacy in Tokyo (Hibiya Park Bldg. 1, 1-8-1 Yurakucho, Chiyoda-ku; Tel. 03/3271-4034), they're much more expensive than back home. If you have special medical needs, it's best to bring an ample supply with you. Japanese pharmacies are called *yakkyoku;* you might also notice *kampoyakkyoku,* which sell traditional herbal remedies.

For urgent dental treatment, go to Oyama Dental Clinic (B-l, Hotel New Otani Arcade, 4-1 Kioicho, Chiyoda-ku, Tokyo; Tel. 03/3221-4182).

HOLIDAYS

On the following holidays, banks and offices will be closed, but stores and restaurants are unaffected. The exception is the New Year period, from 30 December to 3 January, when virtually everything shuts down. Note also that when a holiday falls on a Sunday, the Monday after is also observed as a holiday.

1 January	*New Year's Day*
15 January	*Adults' Day*

11 February	*National Foundation Day*
21 March	*Vernal Equinox Day*
29 April	*Greenery Day*
3 May	*Constitution Day*
5 May	*Children's Day*
15 September	*Respect for the Aged Day*
23 September	*Autumnal Equinox*
10 October	*Health and Sports Day*
3 November	*Culture Day*
23 November	*Labor Thanksgiving Day*
23 December	*Emperor Akihito's Birthday*

If you intend to be in Japan during New Year, Golden Week (29 April to 5 May and adjacent weekends), or the school holidays (March–April and July–August), make your reservations well in advance, as hotels will be full and public transportation more packed than ever. But these periods might be ideal times to visit Tokyo under less crowded conditions — except at New Year, when thousands of provincials flock to the Imperial Palace gardens.

L

LANGUAGE

Unless you already speak good Japanese, it's best to stick to English. It might be fun to exchange a few words or phrases in Japanese for "Thank you," "How are you?" or "Good-bye." But if you give the impression that you're able to take on a fully fledged conversation, you're likely to be swept away by a torrent of incomprehensible syllables instead of the simple communication you really wanted.

Speak slowly and clearly in English, without raising your voice. Try to avoid unnecessary expressions and figures of speech, and instead use the simplest grammar to phrase your questions and answers. The phrases at the back of the book and in the Berlitz phrase book, *Japanese for Travelers,* will help you in situations where you need to speak some Japanese.

M

MAPS

The JNTO provides free tourist maps of Japan, Tokyo, Kyoto/Nara, Fuji, Osaka, and Hokkaido, as well as maps (including location maps) to hotels, *ryokan,* hostels, and railways. All of these are available in English. A road map of Japan, published in English by Buyodo Co., can be found in main bookshops.

MEDIA

Foreign-language magazines, newspapers, and books can be found in large bookshops and hotels. Several daily newspapers are published in English: the *Asahi Evening News,* the *Mainichi Daily News,* the *Japan Times,* and the *Daily Yomiuri,* all on sale at hotels and some newspaper kiosks.

The Far East Network (FEN 810 kHz) broadcasts radio programs in English. Television programs are mostly in Japanese, although news and foreign films are broadcast bilingually on TV sets. Major hotels have satellite TV and English-language cable stations such as CNN.

MONEY

The monetary system is based on the Japanese yen (¥). Coins come in denominations of ¥1, ¥5, ¥10, ¥50, ¥100, and ¥500; banknotes are in ¥1,000, ¥5,000, and ¥10,000 bills. The ¥10 and ¥100 coins are useful for public phones, ¥50 and ¥100 coins for bus tickets, vending machines, and short-distance railway tickets.

Currency exchange. International hotels will change either traveler's checks or foreign currency (if exchange quotations are available) into yen. Accredited banks, of course will do the same — at slightly better rates. With the recent liberalization of financial regulations, stores in many tourist areas are increasingly able to accept payment in currencies other than yen; you will need to present your passport.

When you enter a bank, an employee might greet you and show you the appropriate window. If not, simply look for the relevant sign. You will be invited to sit down while the transaction is being completed, which can take 15 minutes or longer; your name will be called when your money is ready. Most banks have a special foreign-exchange section, where you can change foreign currency and traveler's checks for yen (you must present your passport).

ATMs and credit cards. Despite Japan's financial sophistication, there are very few places where you can use an international credit card and PIN number to make spot cash withdrawals. Since the streets are so safe, however, you can simply take as much cash with you each day as you expect to need for incidentals. For larger expenditures, Visa, American Express, and MasterCard are widely accepted in hotels, inns, restaurants, and shops. Traveler's checks are not.

O

OPEN HOURS

Banks: Open 9am–3pm weekdays; closed on Saturday and Sunday.

Government offices: Open 9am–5pm weekdays; closed Saturday and Sunday.

Barbers and hairdressers: Open 9am–8pm daily except closing days (usually Monday for barbers, Tuesday for hairdressers).

Museums: Open 9am–4:30pm daily except Monday. Most museums are open 9am–5pm on Sunday and National Holidays.

Shops: Most shops open 10am–8pm every day. Department stores are open 10am–7pm weekdays (until 6:30pm or 7pm on Saturday, Sunday, and holidays); they usually close one day during the week.

Temples: Open 8am or 9am to 4:30pm in summer and until 4pm in winter.

P

POLICE

Dial **110** for immediate police assistance or emergencies. There are small police stations or booths *(koban)* on most busy street corners. The police wear a dark blue uniform with a peaked cap. They are extremely courteous and will be ready to help you at any time. You should always present your passport when dealing with the police.

POST OFFICES

Main post offices are open Mon–Fri 8am 7pm, Sat 9am–8pm, and Sun 9am–12:30pm. Local and branch offices are open Mon–Fri 9am–5pm and Sat 9am–12:30pm; they are closed on Sundays. Tokyo International Post Office (Tokyo Kokusai Yubinkyoku, Chiyoda-ku, Otemachi 2-3-3; Tel. 03/3241-4891) is open round the clock for urgent mail.

Stamps are sold at post offices and hotels, as well as at some tobacconists and drugstores. Mail boxes (red for domestic mail, blue for overseas and express mail) are placed on street corners. Some mail boxes have two slots (for domestic and express/international); if you're not sure which to use, either will do. You can also mail letters at hotel desks.

An airmail letter from Japan to any destination in Europe, North America, or Oceania is ¥110 (for ten ounces or less); the rate for a postcard to any place in the world is ¥70. The postal service is fast and reliable.

PUBLIC TRANSPORTATION

Taxis. These are plentiful and readily available at hotels, stations, or airports. Cabs can be flagged down at street corners except in certain locations (such as the Ginza), where they stop only at taxi ranks. They are bright yellow or green and have a lamp on the roof. If the light in the bottom right-hand corner of the windshield is red, the taxi is free; if it's green, it is occupied. The rear doors are remotely controlled by the driver; don't open and close them yourself.

Japan

Few taxi drivers speak English, so have your destination written down on a piece of paper. After 11pm there is a 30 percent surcharge. However, many taxi drivers in Tokyo prefer more lucrative late-night fares than hotel-bound foreigners and might not stop. If you have a problem, ask a Japanese to hail a taxi for you. There is no need to tip taxi-drivers.

Subway. The subway lines in Japanese cities are usually color-coded and easy to use. Trains are frequent, clean, and safe; they run until around midnight. To buy your ticket from the vending machine, first insert coins or notes, then press the button with the fare corresponding to your destination station. If necessary, select another train line that you will change onto, and the fare buttons will change accordingly. Insert your ticket in the automatic ticket barrier, then walk through and pick up your ticket on the other side.

You can buy one-day "open" tickets, which give a day's unlimited travel on the local subways, or (for slightly more) "combination tickets" valid for all trains, subways, and buses. Station platform signs are in Japanese and English; the smaller print at the bottom of the sign indicates the previous and following stations. Avoid the rush-hour crowds (7am–9am and 5pm–7pm).

Bus. A complex network of buses connects most areas of the large cities (in Tokyo it's generally easier to take the subway). Although the destination of the bus is usually written in Japanese only, in Kyoto and Nara there are recorded announcements in English at important stops. You take a ticket from the machine at the rear door when you board, and pay using the driver's machine when you get off. Carry some ¥10 and ¥100 coins with you, although the fare machines usually give change for ¥1000 notes.

Trains. The Japan Railways (JR) network covers the whole country; the trains are clean, safe, and astonishingly punctual. Other private railway networks serve specific regions and are just as much a part of the transportation landscape as JR. (Interestingly, JR trains are often the most expensive and the least comfortable, so always investigate alternative lines in your intended direction.)

JR's world-famous *shinkansen* bullet train has several lines. The fastest *(nozomi)* utilize the newest equipment, and are capable of a white-knuckle 300 km/hr (188 mph) speed.

First-class carriages are called "'green cars" *(greensha)* and are designated by a green four-leaf clover symbol. Most visitors to Japan will benefit hugely from the Japan Railpass, which provides unlimited travel throughout Japan on JR trains (except the *nozomi* super-express bullet train), buses, and the Miyajima ferry. These passes must be bought before arriving in Japan, from Japan Air Lines, JNTO offices, or travel agents.

Air travel. Three main airlines provide extensive regular services connecting the various cities and islands of Japan:

Japan Air Lines (JAL): (03) 5489-2111.

All Nippon Airways (ANA): (03) 5489-8800.

Japan Air System (JAS): (03) 3432-6111.

R

RELIGION

Although Shinto and Buddhism are the major religions, there are over 1,400,000 Christians in Japan, with churches in most towns. However, few services are in English. For the times of Protestant, Catholic, Greek and Russian Orthodox, Muslim, and Jewish services, look at the English-language newspapers or inquire at the local Tourist Information Center.

T

TELEPHONE

For calls originating abroad, first dial the country code for Japan (81), and then the specific city code (Tokyo is 3, Osaka is 6, Yokohama is 45, Kyoto is 75). If you are calling from one Japanese city to another, you must add a 0 before the city code.

International calls through an English-speaking operator can be placed by dialing 0051 from anywhere in Japan.

Japan

Public telephones are differentiated by color and size; all can be used for local, intercity, or long-distance calls. Yellow and green phones can be used for reverse-charge (collect) calls, but not the pink ones (now old and increasingly rare). Large dark-gray telephones marked "ISDN/International & Domestic Card/Coin Telephone" can be used for direct calls. These phones provide high-speed data access and have jacks for modem cables for portable PCs, personal digital assistants, and digital devices, which makes them very convenient for checking e-mail and sending faxes. Instructions are provided in English on an LCD screen.

For domestic calls, NTT phonecards are available from convenience stores, machines, and many shops. Cards are much more convenient than coins, especially since the telephones do not provide change for unused portions of ¥100 coins. However, some (but not all) international pay phones will not let you use an NTT phonecard for international calls, since NTT is not an international carrier. In such cases, you'll need a KDD phonecard. Most international pay phones provide information on international dialing and operator assistance as well as details on which international carriers are available (there are several, all offering similar charges).

Services such as credit calls, reverse-charge (collect) calls, and person-to-person calls are not available for every country, so inquire beforehand. You can also dial direct from KDD (Kokusai Denshin Denwa) offices.

Telegrams and faxes. Overseas telegrams and faxes can be sent from KDD offices (dial 03/3344-5151) or from main post offices. You can also ask for help at the hotel desk. In Tokyo there's a central KDD office at 1-8-1 Otemachi, Chiyoda-ku, Tokyo, 100; Tel. (03) 3275-4343. To send telegrams to addresses within Japan, dial 115. Inland telegrams can also be sent from NTT offices and post offices.

TIME ZONES

Japan is 9 hours ahead of Greenwich Mean Time all year; there is no daylight savings time. The following chart shows the time in various cities in winter:

San Francisco	New York	London	Tokyo	Sydney
4am	7am	noon	9pm	10pm

TIPPING

Tipping isn't customary (unless perhaps if you've requested an extra service) and is officially discouraged. However, a small gift — such as a souvenir of your home town — might be an appreciated gesture for people who have been exceptionally helpful. It is considered courteous to refuse gifts once or twice. Porters at airports and railway stations charge a set fee. Hotels, *ryokan,* and restaurants add a 10%–15% service charge to the bill.

TOILETS

Public toilets are scarce. Use the facilities in department stores, which are generally Western-style, as are those in the big hotels. Japanese-style toilets (most railway stations have them) are floor-level and lack seats: you squat facing the flushing handle. The door usually locks, but it's customary to give two taps on the door to see if the toilet's occupied, if you're inside, you give two taps back. Public toilets are often shared by men and women (men at the urinals are supposed to be ignored). Toilets in Japan are kept scrupulously clean. It's wisest always to carry tissues with you.

TOURIST INFORMATION

The Japan National Tourist Organization (JNTO) operates Tourist Information Centers (TIC) throughout Japan. There are also 16 overseas offices. It provides a wealth of information, including free maps, brochures, tour itineraries, and advice on travel to and within Japan.

For recorded information on major events and entertainment, call JNTO's 24-hour Teletourist service: Tel. (03) 3503-2911 in Tokyo, (075) 361-2911 in Kyoto.

JNTO main office: 2-10-1 Yurakucho, Chiyoda-ku, Tokyo 100-0006.

Tokyo TIC office: B1 Fl., Tokyo International Forum, 3-5-1 Marunouchi, Chiyoda-ku, Tokyo 100-0005; Tel. (03) 3201-3331.

Japan

Narita Airport offices: Terminal 1: Tel. (0476) 32-8711; Terminal 2: (0476) 34-6251.

Kyoto office: Kyoto Tower Bldg., Higashi-Shiokojicho, Shimogyo-ku, Kyoto; Tel. (075) 371-5649.

Australia: Level 33, The Chifley Tower, 2 Chifley Square, Sydney, NSW 2000; Tel. (02) 9232-4522.

Canada: 165 University Ave., Toronto, Ontario MSH 3B8; Tel. (416) 366-7140.

UK: Heathcoat House, 20 Saville Row, London WIX 1AE; Tel. (0171) 734-9638.

US: One Rockefeller Plaza, Suite 1250, New York, NY 10020; Tel. (212) 757-5640.

Travel phone. This system has been devised by the JNTO to help tourists in difficulty, or simply to provide guidance and information. You can call between 9am and 5pm daily from anywhere in the country to connect with English-speaking advisors who can provide whatever help you need. They'll even act as on-the-spot interpreters and translators when necessary. In Tokyo and Kyoto the charge is ¥10 for 3 minutes. Elsewhere, to dial the toll-free numbers you need to insert a ¥10 coin, which will be returned after the call. You can dial the following numbers from any public or private phone.

Tokyo area: (03) 3503-4400.
Eastern Japan (toll free): (0120) 222-800.
Kyoto area: (075) 371-5649.
Western Japan (toll free): (0120) 444-800.

W

WEIGHTS and MEASURES

All the ancient measures have been replaced by the metric system, apart from those used for carpentry in Shinto temples and for making kimono.

Length

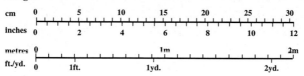

| cm | 0 | 5 | 10 | 15 | 20 | 25 | 30 |
| inches | 0 | 2 | 4 | 6 | 8 | 10 | 12 |

| metres | 0 | | 1m | | 2m |
| ft./yd. | 0 | 1ft. | 1yd. | | 2yd. |

Weight

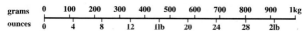

| grams | 0 | 100 | 200 | 300 | 400 | 500 | 600 | 700 | 800 | 900 | 1kg |
| ounces | 0 | 4 | 8 | 12 | 1lb | 20 | 24 | 28 | 2lb | | |

Temperature

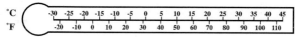

| °C | -30 | -25 | -20 | -15 | -10 | -5 | 0 | 5 | 10 | 15 | 20 | 25 | 30 | 35 | 40 | 45 |
| °F | -20 | -10 | 0 | 10 | 20 | 30 | 40 | 50 | 60 | 70 | 80 | 90 | 100 | 110 | | |

YOUTH HOSTELS

Anyone — whether a member or not — may stay at the public youth hostels run by regional governments. All that's needed is a passport or ID card. To stay at a privately run hostel, you need a valid Youth Hostels Association membership card or an International Guest Card obtainable from Japan Youth Hostels, Inc. Reservations should be made directly to individual hostels (if possible in writing) or by phone, stating name, address, sex, membership card number, length of stay, arrival and departure dates, and meal requirements for the day you arrive. Booking forms are available from the International Youth Hostels Federation.

For further information, contact Japan Youth Hostels: 3rd floor, Hoken Kaikan Bldg., 1-2 Ichigaya-Sadoharacho, Shinjuku-ku, Tokyo 162; Tel. (03) 3269-5831.

Japan

USEFUL EXPRESSIONS

Accommodation

I'd like a single/double room.	shinguru/daburu ruumu o onegai shimas(u)	シングル/ダブルルームをお願いします。
I'd like a room with a bath/shower.	basu/shawa tsuki no heya o onegai shimas(u)	バス/シャワー付の部屋をお願いします。
May I see the room, please?	heya o misete kudasai	部屋を見せてください。

Communications

Where's the nearest telephone?	ichiban chikai denwa wa doka des(u) ka	いちばん近い電話はどこですか。
I'd like to send a message by e-mail/fax.	denshi-meeru/fakk(u)su de messeeji o okuritain des(u) ga	電子メール/ファックスでメッセージを送りたいんですが。
I'd like a telephone card, please.	terehon kaado o kudasai	テレホンカードをください。

Customs and Entry Regulations

I have only the normal allowances.	menzee no han-i nai shika arimasen	免税の範囲内しかありません。

Emergencies

Call the police!	keesatsu o yonde	警察を呼んで！
Get a doctor!	isha o yonde	医者を呼んで！
Help!	tas(u)kete	助けて！
I'm lost.	michi ni mayoi mash(i)ta	道に迷いました。

Language tips (General)

Good morning.	ohayoo gozaimas(u)	おはようございます。
Good afternoon.	kon-nichi-wa	こんにちは。
Good evening.	konban wa	こんばんは。
Good night.	oyasumi nasai	おやすみなさい。
Good-bye.	sayoonara	さようなら。
Please.	doozo/onegai shimas(u)	どうぞ。/お願いします。

Thank you.	arigatoo	ありがとう。
You're welcome.	doozo	どうぞ。
Yes/No.	hai/iie	はい。/いいえ。
Excuse me.	sumimasen	すみません。
I don't understand.	wakarimasen	分かりません。
How much is that?	ikura des(u) ka	いくらですか。

Lost Property

I've lost my …	… o nak(u)shi mash(i)ta	…をなくしました。
wallet/handbag/ passport	saifu/hando baggu/ pas(u)pooto	財布/ハンドバッグ/ パスポート

Money Matters

I want to change some money.	o kane o kaetain des(u) ga	お金を替えたいんですが。
I want to cash some traveller's checks [cheques].	toraberaazu chekku o kankin sh(i)tain des(u) ga	トラベラーズチェックを 換金したいんですが。
Where are the ATMs [cash machines]?	kyasshu koonaa wa doko des(u) ka	キャッシュコーナーは どこですか。

Numbers

One	ichi	一		Twenty	ni-juu	二十
Two	ni	二		Thirty	san-juu	三十
Three	san	三		Ninety	kyuu-juu	九十
Four	shi/yon	四				
Five	go	五				
Six	roku	六		One hundred	hyaku	百
Seven	shichi/nana	七				
Eight	hachi	八		One thousand	sen	千
Nine	kyuu/ku	九				
Ten	juu	十				

Counting objects/items

One	hitotsu	一つ		Six	muttsu	六つ
Two	futatsu	二つ		Seven	nanatsu	七つ
Three	mittsu	三つ		Eight	yattsu	八つ
Four	yottsu	四つ		Nine	kokonotsu	九つ
Five	itsutsu	五つ		Ten	too	十

Restaurants

A table for ..., please.	... onegai shimas(u)	...お願いします。
How much is that?	ikura des(u) ka	いくらですか。

Asking the Waiter

The bill (check), please.	o-kanjoo onegai shimas(u)	お勘定、お願いします。
I'd like ...	... o kudasai	...をください。
fish	sakana	魚
beef	gyuu	牛
pork	buta	豚
chicken	tori	鶏
bread	pan	パン
potatoes	poteto/bareesho	ポテト/馬鈴薯
rice	gohan	ご飯
salad	sarada	サラダ
Japanese pickled vegetables	tsukemono	漬物
soup	suupu	スープ
vegetables	yasai	果物
fruit	kudamono	野菜
pepper	koshoo	コショウ
salt	shio	塩
sugar	satoo	砂糖
water	mizu	水
coffee	koohii	コーヒー
tea	koocha	紅茶
wine	wain	ワイン
beer	biirru	ビール
Japanese sake	nihonshu	日本酒

Reading the Menu

bean-paste soup	miso shiro	みそ汁
grilled fish	yaki zakana	焼き魚
fried rice with pork	chaahan	炒飯
deep-fried shrimp and vegetables	tenpura	天ぷら

beef steamboat	shabu shabu	しゃぶしゃぶ
sliced beef and vegetables	sukiyaki	すき焼
thin buckwheat noodles	soba	そば
thick wheat-flour noodles	udon	うどん
chilled noodles	hiyamugi	冷麦
noodles in broth with tempura	tenpura udon	天ぷらうどん
Chinese noodles in a broth	ramen	ラーメン
savory pancakes	okonomiyaki	お好み焼き
bean curd	tofu	豆腐
rice balls wrapped in seaweed	temaki zushi	手巻き寿司
deep-fried pork cutlet	ton katsu	とんかつ

Sushi

assorted raw fish	sashimi moriawase	刺身盛り合わせ
tuna	maguro	鮪/マグロ
salmon	sake	鮭/サケ
prawn	ebi	海老/エビ

Taxi

Where can I get a taxi?	tak(u)shii wa doko de nore mas(u) ka	タクシーはどこで乗れますか。
How much will it cost?	ikura ni narimas(u) ka	いくらになりますか。

Trains

How do I get to the train station?	eki niwaa doo yatte ikemas(u) ka	駅には、どうやって行けますか。
Where is the ticket office?	kippu uriba wa doko des(u) ka	きっぷうりばはどこですか。
one-way/round trip	katamichi/oofuku	片道/住復

Toilets

Where are the toilets?	toire wa doko des(u) ka	トイレはどこですか。
Ladies	josee	女性
Gentlemen	dansee	男性

Tourist Information

Where is the tourist office?	kankoo an-nai-jo doko des(u) ka	観光案内所はどこですか。
Do you have any information on …?	… no an-nai wa arimas(u) ka	…の案内はありますか。
Are there any trips to …?	… e no tsuaa wa arimas(u) ka	…へのツアーは ありますか。
How much does the tour cost?	sono tsuaa wa ikura des(u) ka	そのツアーはいくら ですか。
Do you have a guide book?	gaido-bukku wa arimas(u) ka	ガイドブックは ありますか。
Can you help me?	tas(u)kete kudasai	助けてください。

Place Names and Attractions

Akihabara	akihabara	秋葉原
Arashiyama	arashiyama	嵐山
Asakusa: Sensoji Temple and Denbo-in	asakusa: sensoo-ji to denboo-in	浅草：浅草寺と伝法院
Chubu	chuubu	中部
Daisen'in	daisen-in	大仙院
Dotomburi	dootonbori	道頓堀
Fushimi-Inari shrine	fushimi inari taisha	伏見稲荷大社
Ginkakuji Temple	ginkaku-ji	銀閣寺
Ginza	ginza	銀座
Gion	gion	祇園
Hakone	hakone	箱根
Heian Shrine	heean jinguu	平安神宮
Himeji	himeji	姫路
Himeji Castle	himeji-joo	姫路城
Hiroshima	hiroshima	広島
Hokkaido	hokkaidoo	北海道
Honshu	honshuu	本州
Horyuji Temple	hooryuu-ji	法隆寺
Koko-en	kooko-en	好古園

Imperial Palace: East Garden, Nijubashi Bridge and Sakuradamon Gate	kookyo: higashi gyoen, nijuu-bashi, sakurada-mon	皇居：東御苑、二重橋、桜田門
Ise-shima	ise-shima	伊勢志摩
Itsukushima/"Floating" torii	its(u)kushima jinja	厳島神社
Izu Peninsula	izu hantoo	伊豆半島
Kamakura	kamakura	鎌倉
Kanazawa	kanazawa	金沢
Kansai	kansai	関西
Kanto	kantoo	関東
Kappabashi	kappa-bashi	河童橋
Kasuga Grand Shrine	kasuga taisha	春日大社
Katsura Imperial Villa	katsura rikyuu	桂離宮
Kenrokuen Park	kenrokuen	兼六園
Kiyomizu Temple	kiyomizu-dera	清水寺
Kobe	koobe	神戸
Koyasan	kooya-san	高野山
Kurashiki	kurashiki	倉敷
Kyoto	kyooto	京都
Kyushu	kyuushuu	九州
Meiji Jingu and Harajuku	meeji jinguu to harajuku	明治神宮と原宿
Miho Museum	miho bijutsu-kan	Miho美術館
Miyajima	miyajima	宮島
Mt. Fuji	fuji-san	富士山
Nagasaki	nagasaki	長崎
Nara	nara	奈良
Nara Park	nara kooen	奈良公園
Nezu Institute of Fine Arts	nezu bijutsu-kan	根津美術館
Nigatsu-do	nigatsu-doo	二月堂
Nijo Castle	nijoo-joo	二条城
Nikko	nikkoo	日光

Nishi-Honganji Temple	nishi hongan-ji	西本願寺
Osaka	oosaka	大阪
Osaka Castle	oosaka-joo	大阪城
Peace Memorial Museum	heewa kinen-kan	平和記念館
Peace Park	heewa kinen kooen	平和記念公園
Philosopher's Path	tetsugaku no michi	哲学の道
Ryoanji	ryooan-ji	竜安寺
Sanzen'in Temple	sanzen-in	三千院
Shinsaibashi shopping arcade	shinsai-bashi suji shootengai	心斎橋筋商店街
Shikoku	shikoku	四国
Shinjuku: Metropolitan Government Office	shinjuku: tookyoo tochoo	新宿：東京都庁
Takayama	takayama	高山
Todaiji Temple	toodai-ji	東大寺
Tohoku	toohoku	東北
Toji Temple	too-ji	東寺
Toyako Spa	tooya-ko onsen	洞爺湖温泉
Tokyo	tookyoo	東京
Tsukiji Central Wholesale Fish Market	tsukiji uo ichiba (chuuoo oroshiuri ichiba)	築地魚市場 (中央卸売市場)
Ueno: Ken'eiji, Tokyo National Museum, and Toshogu	ueno: kan'ee-ji, tookyoo kokuritsu hakubutsu-kan, tooshoguu	上野：寛永寺、東京国立博物館、東照宮
Wakayama	wakayama	和歌山
Yufuin	yufuin	由布院 or 湯布院
Yokohama	yokohama	横浜